PRAISE

The Unspoken F

"This book is like fresh-baked bread. My spiritual mouth watered as the aroma of its fresh revelation filled my life. I am making this book must-eating for every hungry single and un-single person in my church."

—GILBERT A. THOMPSON, presiding bishop of Church Without Walls International and senior pastor of New Covenant Christian Church in Boston, Massachusetts

"Got love on your mind? Then you would do well to know *The Unspoken Rules of Love*. Michelle and Joel have taken an honest and transparent look at the relationship between man and woman and have given us fourteen rules to guide us into healthy, long-lasting relationships."

—ALICIA WILLIAMSON, author of *A Seeking Heart: Rediscovering True Worship*

"I believe this book will be a vital tool in transforming the way unmarried people view wholeness and fulfillment in life. Joel and Michelle do a wonderful job of addressing the issues, deceptions, and fears that many single women face, and how they must position themselves to receive God's best."

—ROBB THOMPSON, senior pastor of Family Harvest Church International in Tinley Park, Illinois

BUSARA · BOOKS

The unspoken rules of Love

WHAT WOMEN DON'T KNOW AND MEN DON'T TELL YOU

MICHELLE McKINNEY HAMMOND

JOEL A. BROOKS Jr.

WATERBROOK
PRESS

THE UNSPOKEN RULES OF LOVE
PUBLISHED BY WATERBROOK PRESS
2375 Telstar Drive, Suite 160
Colorado Springs, Colorado 80920
A division of Random House, Inc.

ISBN 1-57856-671-1

Published in association with the literary agency of Alive Communications, Inc., 7680 Goddard Street, Suite 200, Colorado Springs, Colorado 80920.

Library of Congress Cataloging-in-Publication Data
Brooks, Joel A.
     The unspoken rules of love : what women don't know and men don't tell you / by Joel A. Brooks Jr. and Michelle McKinney Hammond.— 1st ed.
          p. cm.
Includes bibliographical references.
     ISBN 1-57856-671-1
     1. Single women—Religious life. 2. Christian women—Religious life. 3. Love—Religious aspects—Christianity. 4. Mate selection—Religious aspects—Christianity. I. McKinney Hammond, Michelle, 1957– II. Title.
     BV4596.S5 B76 2003
     306.7—dc21

                                                                2002152721

Printed in the United States of America
2003—First Edition

10 9 8 7 6 5 4 3 2 1

from Joel A. Brooks Jr.:

To my twin daughters, Victoria and Veronica. My desire to prepare you for life as single adult women was the inspiration that led me to seek out the information that I share in this book.

I am very proud of you.

from Michelle McKinney Hammond:

To all those who have done it wrong, are still trying to get it right, as well as those who have lived to laugh at their mistakes and move on to better tomorrows: The essential secret to living and loving is to leave the past where you left it and to embrace tomorrow with new hope in one hand and wisdom in the other. I wish you rivers of love that will carry you to your heart's desire.

Contents

Contents

Use Your Head, Girl!

Even as you reached for it, you thought to yourself, *Do I need this? What unspoken rules?*

This book would never have caught your eye if you didn't need to learn these rules. You would never have responded to the Spirit within, the still small voice that said, "Go on, Girl, that's the one you need. Go ahead and get it. As a matter of fact, do not stop, do not pass go, do not collect two hundred dollars. Life is not a game, so get it now!"

We say good for you! A desire for more wisdom is healthy. It means you want results—and not the ones you've *been* getting. You want *different* results. As women we spend an awful lot of time dissecting the male psyche without any input from them, so I've enlisted the help of one of the wisest men I know, Joel Brooks, to help me break it down. One way or another we are going to make love work. But it begins when we stop making the same mistakes based on the wrong assumptions. Someone once said that we don't change until the cost of staying the same exceeds the cost of change. No one can keep sowing the same old seeds and expect to reap a different harvest. Yet many women have the same type of relationship with men over and over again, all of which come to the same disappointing end. The common cry is "What's wrong with me?"

For those of us who don't want to examine ourselves, the defensive answer is "There is absolutely nothing wrong with me. It's all *his* fault." We do a role reversal with Adam in the garden. Remember when God confronted Adam and Eve after they had eaten the fruit? Eve blamed the serpent. Adam said it was Eve's fault, as well as God's fault, for giving him the woman in the first place. At the end of the conversation, God didn't let Adam slide. He said Adam was wrong for listening to her! Oops! Guess it was everybody's bad.

It's interesting to note that the serpent didn't even try to deny his part in the drama. It must be human to blame.

The truth of the matter is, when two people fail to sustain a relationship, both had something to do with its demise. It's time to stop namin' and blamin' and time to start dealing with ourselves. The only person you can control or change is you. For those new to the relationship game, this is your opportunity to start off on the right foot. Our goal is that you read this book and apply the principles, so that if you are not in a committed relationship, it will be only because of God's perfect timing and plan for your life, not because of anything you're doing or failing to do. No matter how together you are, timing is still everything. If that man isn't totally ready emotionally, spiritually, or mentally, he can wound you in ways that will make your marriage difficult in the beginning. That is, if you are even able to get past the unnecessary relationship dramas to marry him in the first place.

WHY ARE THE RULES OF LOVE UNSPOKEN?

Paul said that when he was a child he spoke like a child, he thought like a child, and he reasoned like a child, but when he became a man he put childish ways behind him (see 1 Corinthians 13:11). The childish ways he referred to had to do with the subject of love. He had finally learned what true love was. Paul learned that true love is more about *giving* than *getting,* that mature love seeks the welfare of the other person first. Unconditional, sacrificial love endures through all things. This outlook involves a mind decision more than a heart condition or feeling. He changed his approach to love, and therefore, the response he received also changed. It seems that, based on 1 Corinthians 13 (the love chapter) and subsequent writings, Paul spent a great deal of time pondering the concept of love and came to some very clear conclusions about what it was and what it was not. He was grappling with God's concept of unconditional *agape* love versus the other forms of love—*phileo,* or brotherly love, and *eros,* sexual love.

Paul was not alone in his pondering on this subject. We, too, struggle with the dynamics of what makes love work between a man and a woman. Why don't we discuss this today? Why are the rules of love for the most part unspoken? Because they are not really considered—everyone enjoys *feeling* instead of *thinking*. Much is said about love and about how to relate to one another, but the surface conclusions concerning how to relate person-to-person do not work in a love relationship because men and women are different. Even worse, to cite those differences as realities is currently politically incor-

WISE UP

As you begin to gain wisdom and balance your heart (emotions) with your head (mind), some of your habits will change and some folks won't understand. Expect the likelihood of a little resistance to the new you.

Your mother, for example, might want you to do things the way she did them. She may not see her ways as unhealthy. Many have suffered the death of a love relationship due to habits that seemed natural and normal but were unacceptable to the other partner. "But why didn't he like that? What was wrong with it? I thought everybody did that. Well, I don't know what happened at *his* house when *he* was growing up, but that's the way my family did it!" God does say to honor your parents, but it isn't always wise to follow their behavioral patterns.

Your friends may also want you to agree with their way of seeing things. They, too, may not realize that their thought patterns are wrong. The changes in you may even issue a silent challenge

rect. So in this environment, we are unable to set forth any workable guidelines for male-female interaction. We just don't talk about it. We go with the flow, which usually means we never reach our desired destination—Love City.

A woman must take into account her emotional makeup and her inclination toward relational love, which in a marriage and family

that they should examine themselves and make some changes of their own.

But your decision to approach relationships with wisdom has nothing to do with mothers or others. This is about you, about changing your life for the better. From this moment forward, decide to make wise choices. You are free to follow God's advice about every area of your life, including your love life. As you adhere to the Bible's laws and decrees, you will find your love relationships coming alive!

Once you wise up, live it, don't say it. Simply consider the ways of men and decide whether they should remain in your life and, if so, in what role. Do not tear down others or crush their spirits. Do not bury anyone's self-esteem. If exits are necessary, be graceful.

Remain on your guard. A little bit of knowledge can be dangerous. It can fool you into believing you know everything. When your nose is in the air, you run the risk of stumbling over another bad decision because you weren't looking where you should—at yourself.

setting is often the strength of that unit. The same strength, however, is often a weakness for single women. When a single woman longs for a relationship, her desire makes her vulnerable. If desire overrides wisdom, her predisposition often becomes the root of bad decisions. Wisdom and discipline must accompany this wonderful loving heart that God gave a woman.

Most women do not want to use their heads when it comes to love. They want to let love take its own course and see where it carries them. This is dangerous. So often a woman gives her heart too soon, then spends her time trying to recapture the feeling the man gave her when they first became involved.

Another reason the rules are unspoken is because men unconsciously and sometimes consciously take advantage of what women don't know about themselves, about men, and how their differences affect their relationships. In this case, what you don't know will definitely hurt you. The man who is aware of these truths and has wrong motives can manipulate and lead a woman along, never intending to commit or to allow the relationship to go where he knows the woman wants it to. The man who is unaware of these unspoken rules will find himself puzzled at the end of a relationship by the woman's disappointment and heartbreak, wondering, *What did I do?* Also, a well-meaning man can be sincerely surprised when he discovers that he isn't meeting a woman's unspoken expectations. He may find himself pulling away from someone he was initially attracted to because of a pattern of misunderstanding.

When dealing with love, we tend to spiritualize it or feel our way through it, and we don't use our head! Have you ever been to someone's home and found yourself feeling disoriented by the way the furniture was arranged? Did it make you ill at ease? Did you cut your visit short, not caring to remain? Your thought life is like this room: Wrong thinking creates attitudes that make a candidate for a love relationship uncomfortable. Some of us need to rearrange the furniture in our minds and hearts so that the right guest will be happy to remain.

To do this, we've got to have wisdom. Now let's talk about that. While some say ignorance is bliss, don't believe the hype. What you don't know *will* hurt you—and keep on hurting you until you learn your lessons. Wisdom will keep you safe and make you happier than you thought possible! So agree to live and learn. With all your getting, get understanding and follow after what you have learned.

An often-overlooked passage of Scripture is well worth consideration. (If you are not one who gleans nuggets from the Bible as guideposts for your life, please bear with us. Whether you have chosen to anchor your faith in God or not, the Scriptures are still universal law. Whether you believe them or not, they still work.) We've made a composite of these verses from several translations so you can get the full impact of what is being said.

> Know this, that in the last days will come times that are hard to deal with and hard to bear because men will be lovers of themselves and utterly self-centered. Lovers of money, greedy, aroused by an inordinate desire for

wealth, boastful, proud and arrogant, abusive, disobedient to their parents, ungrateful, and unholy. They will be without natural affection or love, callous, unforgiving, slanderous, troublemakers, without self-control, loose in morals and conduct, brutal, hostile and unfriendly to good men (or women).

They will be treacherous, rash, conceited, lovers of sensual pleasures and vain amusements rather than lovers of God. They will go to church, yes, and maintain a facade of religion, but they will resist its influence and deny and reject the power of it. Avoid all such people. For among them are those who worm their way into the homes and captivate *silly* women and weak-natured, spiritually dwarfed women, loaded down with sins and easily swayed and led away by various evil desires and seductive impulses. (See 2 Timothy 3:1-6)

That's a mouthful but easy to break down to where we really live. It's talking about false teachers who were leading newly converted women astray from the truths they had learned. This also can apply to men who seduce women today. Do you know any men like the ones mentioned in the sentence above? Come on, tell the truth and shame the devil. We *all* do.

The desire for love is a God-given desire. However, when it becomes an obsession, it quickly turns to idolatry, which is evil and attracts more evil—men who aren't good. The men referred to in these verses took advantage of women who were silly, weak, and led by their desires because they lacked spiritual strength. Are you beginning to see the picture? Uh-huh, they lacked wisdom. Therefore they were open to anything. Wisdom gives you safe boundaries and protects you from men whose intentions are not honorable.

Proverbs gives an account of a man who is seduced by an adulterous woman. Check it out in context with the roles reversed:

> I was looking out the window of my house one day and saw a simple-minded young woman who lacked common sense. She was crossing the street near the house of an immoral man. She was strolling down the path by his house at twilight, as the day was fading, as the dark of night set in. The man approached her, dressed seductively and sly of heart. He was the brash, rebellious type who never stays at home. He is often seen in the streets and markets, soliciting at every corner. He threw his arms around her and kissed her, and with a brazen look he said, "…It's you I was looking for! I came to find you and here you are!… Come let's drink our fill of love until morning. Let's enjoy each other's caresses.…" So he seduced her with his pretty speech. With his flattery he enticed her.
>
> She followed him at once, like an ox going to the slaughter or like a trapped deer, awaiting the arrow that would pierce her heart. She was like a bird flying into a

snare, little knowing it would cost her her life. Listen to me, my daughters, and pay attention to my words. Don't let your hearts stray away toward him. Don't wander down his wayward path. For he has been the ruin of many; numerous women have been his victims. His house is the road to the grave. His bedroom is the den of death. (see Proverbs 7:6-13,15,18,21-27, NLT)

My, my, my! Can you believe all of this is in the Bible! This is serious stuff, but we know you can relate. Many women have met a smooth operator and known he was trouble with a capital *T*. Despite this knowledge, they've allowed themselves to be seduced and their hearts to be broken. This destruction can happen when their hopes for true love are fading over the horizon of their longings, and they decide that something is better than nothing: We settle for less than God's best for us. All because of a lack of wisdom or the refusal to heed it.

In Proverbs 9, Wisdom and Folly are personified as women. But just as there is a thin line between love and hate, there is a thin line between wisdom and folly, or foolishness, and it is easy to err. Folly personifies everything that Wisdom is not. Folly pursues men, is loud, ignorant, and deceptive. She is constantly bringing ruin on herself. "The wise woman builds her house, but with her own hands the foolish one tears hers down" (Proverbs 14:1). In other words, the foolish woman comes undone by her own doing.

Wisdom is gracious and inviting to everyone, stable and honest about her intentions. She is consistent and immovable because her house is built on a firm foundation and supported with seven pillars that give her strength: prudence, knowledge, discretion, sound judgment, understanding, and power (see Proverbs 8:12-14). Not her own power, but the power that comes from above. She does not lean on her own understanding or allow her feelings to guide her. Instead she follows the leading of the Spirit of God.

The subtle danger of making choices is that Wisdom and Folly both make their appeal to you from the same place: the high place. To unspiritualize this, we mean your mind. They are both in clear view. They both call out invitations to come and visit. You are invited to eat and drink what each of them serves, but the end of the evening will be very different depending on whose party you choose to attend. If you choose to embrace Wisdom, you gain all kinds of benefits—long, good life, riches, honor, justice, and fair treatment. But make friends with Folly and suffer the death of all you hold dear: Shattered dreams and broken hearts are the door prizes at Folly's affair.

We've been told over and over to follow our hearts, yet we must be careful. God gave us a heart and a mind. We must balance the two. The heart can be a spoiled brat, wanting what it wants and wanting it right now. Caught up in the moment, the heart does not consider the consequences. The heart chooses, but the head must qualify the choice. You can feel right about the wrong thing. Listen to your heart, but use your head to sift its information. Your heart does not own you; neither should it control you. Instead, you must learn to master your heart.

Follow and embrace wisdom like a sister. Make insight a beloved member of your family. They will keep you grounded, safe, and whole. Cherish the wisdom you receive, hold it close, treasure it like a true friend, and consult with it often until wisdom becomes a natural way of life. That's when the fun will start and you will find yourself on the path to living and loving as never before.

I Have No Man

Rule #1: Take Your Life Off of Hold

A country could be run on the energy some women put into end-lessly thinking about and discussing how to reach marital status quick, fast, and in a hurry before the biological clock strikes mid-night. Their energy is not spent on living a purposeful life, and the joy that other areas of life offer is ignored, for the most part. We call this common disease one-tree-itis—concentrating on the one thing you don't have while missing the enjoyment from everything else that *is* at your disposal. The mother of all women, Eve, suffered from one-tree-itis and fell from grace. Ignoring all of her other options for satisfaction, she ate the fruit from the one forbidden tree.

Many women have decided, assumed, or been taught that true happiness comes through a relationship with a man. So they postpone their happiness and wholeness until the right man shows up in their life. When they talk about happiness or wholeness, they immediately mention the man who isn't there or their partner who isn't right. They may even feel they have a good excuse for being unproductive in other areas of their lives—on which the presence or absence of a man has no bearing.

Are you feeling as if God is holding out on you, refusing to give you a mate, not paying attention to your needs or desires? Are you feeling like a woman's got to do what a woman's got to do in order to get what she wants? Are you feeling as if taking matters into your own hands is a better gamble than waiting any longer on God's divine timing?

You can wait so long for something you think will bring you happiness that *waiting* actually replaces the pursuit of happiness. As you fix your gaze on that one desire, you postpone or miss your happiness because you don't recognize present opportunities for joy.

I HAVE NO MAN

Here's an example. There was a pool called Bethesda whose stirring waters healed. The disciple John said (in John 5) that the pool had five porches and that it was filled with people who were blind, lame, or paralyzed. Any one of these physical conditions would describe the state of a woman who can't see a clear picture of a happy future unless there is a man in it. Some just don't have the capacity or the energy to walk through life solo. Others are stuck in waiting mode, unable to get on with the business of living or securing anything of lasting value without a partner.

There was one man who had been lying there sick for thirty-eight years. Thirty-eight years! Can you imagine? Yet many women have been sick from the lack of love for more years than they care to relate.

Anyway, Jesus showed up on the scene and approached the paralyzed man. Jesus knew how long he had been ill and asked him what seems like an unnecessary question: "Would you like to get well?" or, as another translation says, "Do you want to be whole?" Now how would you respond to that question if you were in this man's situation? You would say, "Yes! Of course I do!" But that is not what the man said. He replied, "I can't, sir. Because I have *no man* to help me into the pool when the water is stirred up. While I am trying to get there, someone else always gets in ahead of me." Sound familiar? For women, the version goes something like this: "I can't be whole and I can't be completely happy, because every time I have a chance at love something happens. Everybody's got someone but me. Everybody else is getting married before me. If I have to wear one more bridesmaid dress, I will scream."

The setup of this scenario gives us a hint at some deeper truths. It's important to note that Jesus addressed the man with a question that seemingly had an obvious answer. God's questions are often designed not to extract answers but to provoke thought. When Adam and Eve hid in the garden after messing up, God asked Adam, "Where are you?" God already knew where Adam was. He wanted Adam to think about where he was. *I made you whole. I put you in the Garden where you had everything you needed. I told you one thing not to do and told you what would happen when you did it. You did that one thing. It happened. Now where are you?* God was asking, "Where is your head, or what are you thinking now? Now that you have done what you thought would make you whole and it hasn't, where are you? What is your mind-set at this point?" God is much more concerned that we learn to become obedient than with our mistake or sin.

What do you really want in life? List five things that you want. Look at your list and ask yourself if it would be possible to have these things and still be unhappy. If that is possible, you are focusing on the wrong list and are on the wrong path to happiness.

Let's look again at the question Jesus asked: "Do you want to be made whole?" Clearly something was wrong with this man; brokenness was apparent, yet Jesus didn't deal with the problem or make a diagnosis. He simply asked the man his desire. Are your desires birthed out of brokenness? Are the things on your list meant to complete you? Or are they a list of desires recorded by a person who is already complete? This man's need was obvious, but Jesus asked him what he wanted. Ask yourself if your desire for a love relationship comes from a sense of brokenness or from feeling incomplete.

WAITING IN VAIN?

Now let's look at the Bethesda man's problems. This man had been at the place of healing for a long time. He was paralyzed. In order to obtain healing he has to be the *first* one in the pool after the troubling of the water. Without assistance he would never make it to the pool, and even with assistance, what were his chances of getting there first? It's safe to say no well person was going to wait with him. After all, would a person really wait at the pool among all that sickness if they were whole themselves?

No other sick person was going to help him either. Wouldn't the other ill people try to get into the pool first? Anyone with an infirmity that didn't involve paralysis would certainly beat him to the pool. Realistically, the paralyzed man's chances of becoming whole at the pool were close to impossible, yet he waited day after day because that was the only way he thought he could obtain healing.

When was the last time you met a good man and felt so generous you decided to introduce him to one of your other single friends? Mmm hmm. It was all about making a love connection *yourself*, wasn't it? How many married women you know consistently hang out with single women? Probably not many. They are occupied elsewhere, protecting and enjoying what is precious to them.

So single women are resigned to a cynical belief that there are no men qualified for marriage (they're taken), while at the same time they longingly wait for that special man to come along. This frame of mind leads to two equally depressing emotions: despair and desperation. Both can have disastrous effects on a woman, not the least of which sets a woman up for one of her biggest problems—compromise, which we will discuss later.

Look at your list again. Are the items on your happiness list those that bring you happiness or what you believe you *need* in order to be happy? Many people mistake a means to happiness as happiness itself. The paralyzed man originally came to the pool to be healed but having been there so long waiting, the object of his longing became "someone to help him" rather than his healing.

Happiness is a part of being whole. It means having an understanding of your identity and purpose, an established feeling of acceptance and value, and a sense of destiny, joy, and peace—all of which produce overall well-being. It is impossible to be consistently happy without these characteristics. All people need to know who they are, why they are here, and to whom they belong. Having an understanding of who we are in Christ is foundational to the belief system that allows you to possess these qualities. The Bible says in Romans 14:17 that the kingdom of God is righteousness, peace, and joy *in the Holy Spirit.* You find in this passage all these characteristics that grow out of being in right relationship with God. His presence is always accompanied by peace and joy; in other words, a sense of total well-being.

FILLING THE VOID

Let's take a deeper look at the concept of wholeness. We are told in Colossians 2:10 that "you are complete through your union with Christ" (NLT).

"Well how can that be?" you ask. "Jesus can't show up and take me to dinner. He can't hold me or deal with my physical needs…"

But wholeness comes from within. It does not rely on outward stimuli or circumstances that constantly shift. When you know who you are, nothing can change your heart condition except you.

Knowing who we are requires filling that God-sized void in us that only God can fill. We were never meant to be apart from God. To be separated from him is to be incomplete. In the Garden of Eden, man was made whole, but he was also created with a built-in dependence upon God. The whole capacity that a man or woman has to experience pleasure and to feel good is God's idea—even the word *eden* means pleasure. Yet because Adam and Eve chose independence

LET GOD RULE

A pregnant woman quickly discovers, as her pregnancy progresses, that she is no longer in control of her body. The new life inside of her begins to rule. Favorite foods no longer agree with her system. She has to change the position she sleeps in. Her clothing has to change to accommodate her new shape. She is definitely not in control.

When we make up our minds that we want a new life, we can no longer do things the same way we used to do them. Our habits must change to allow the new life we crave to be formed within us. We should be willing to make these changes because we anticipate great things coming from the new life.

God wants to give us new life. He wants to give us new love lives, but we must be willing to allow God to rule.

and sinned following that decision, mankind became unsafe and inse-cure. Adam and Eve lost their joy, peace, and identity, and began their own course of trying to make themselves whole. We've been attempt-ing to fix ourselves without consulting our Maker ever since.

Every day we read any number of different magazines and self-help books, all doling out prescriptions and remedies for making ourselves whole without the help of God, even though some allude to a higher power or supreme being. But God will make us whole in a much more purposeful and precise way. Unlike what this worldly advice offers, his solution is a permanent one with lasting effects. One amazing dose of God's prescription for overall well-being— faith in Jesus—will restore our connection to him. Isn't it incredible that one broken life can make countless others whole? Jesus, the Son of God, came to save us (John 3:16). To *sozo* us, as the original Greek infers, means to make us whole, to give us a sense of contentment, to save us from bondage and destruction. God's desire is to give us wholeness.

When we receive Christ as our Savior, our spirit is reborn. The renewing of our mind begins the transformation that leads us to wholeness. When our mind begins to think a new way, our emotions must be harnessed and our will must yield to a new and different set of instructions that will be contrary to popular world standards. God's way to wholeness is truly different—and permanent. The world offers countless paths to reach that coveted place called whole-ness, but each one ultimately leads to an unsatisfactory dead end.

For example, the world tells us that we can define our identity by what we do. We are human *beings,* though, not human *doings,* so while our vocation can help us feel good about ourselves, it can never make us whole. The same is true of money and high-end clothing. If you have a lot, you may feel safe, secure, and whole. But money and material possessions cannot provide what God was meant to provide.

Neither can wholeness come from a relationship. A woman learns from a young age that a man—her knight in shining armor—will come along and make everything all right. He will sweep her up and rescue her from her doldrums and boredom, then bring her into a new life. This happily-ever-after is an illusion. Relationships cannot provide what God was meant to provide.

THE KEY TO HAPPINESS

Now let's qualify that statement. There is the capacity for happiness in a relationship between a man and a woman that is not available to a single person. There is also a possible *misery* that people who are *not* in relationships do not experience. Ed Cole, author of *Maximized Manhood,* said that marriage is the closest thing to heaven or hell that you can find on earth. Marriage is not the key to happiness. God would not base our wholeness on something that requires another person's participation. It is God's ideal that married people share one hope and spirit, treat each other with love, serve each other, and respect each other, so that marriage is an awesome relationship that brings joy to the participants and glorifies God. However, when mates have different values and lack mutual respect, they will have difficulty serving one another. For this reason more people are, unfortunately, enduring hurting relationships rather than enjoying healthy ones.

We make bad decisions because of a flawed belief system. Wrong beliefs lead to inaccurate conclusions, which are the basis for wrong decisions, ultimately sending us in the wrong direction. The illusion that was painted for Adam and Eve is still being presented to us today—that we can be independent of God, make our own judgments, make our own decisions, and still be whole. This line of thinking was proven wrong from the beginning of time and continues to carry us further and further away from the wholeness we crave.

One of the qualities that successful people have is focus. Focus is the ability to cut out distractions and concentrate on one thing. But, the negative side to focus is tunnel vision, focusing on something to the point that you don't see other things. Many in their pursuit of happiness or love have focused so much on relationships with the opposite sex that they miss the other opportunities for pleasure, joy, and the wholeness that God provides.

Noted author and teacher Mike Murdock states that whatever has distracted you has mastered you. On too many occasions, while on the road to wholeness, we get distracted by the things we were taught would make us whole. Just as our friend did that Jesus found lying by the pool. *In his mind,* his wholeness was based on a person. Are you lying by the same pool? What will be your answer when Jesus asks, "Do you want to be whole?" Surely you can think of a better answer than "I have no man."

Things That Make You Go Hmmm...

- What is on your list of requirements for happiness?

- What do you feel is keeping you from being a whole person? Have you ever felt whole without whatever it may be?

- What influences have formed your ideal for wholeness? Are they reliable sources?

Chapter Two

Five Husbands and Still Thirsty

Rule #2: Remove the Obstacles to Wholeness

Women fall into very different categories regarding the longing for love. The first is "I have no man." The second is "I have had one man too many." Varying lines of reason in this second category include the "Hey, someone is better than no one" way of thinking, which can lead to a succession of relationships with the wrong type of men. And there is the "Since there is a shortage of men, I'm not opposed to sharing" group. Then there are those who have suffered so much disappointment with men that they now seek consolation in the arms of other women. All of these responses of the heart spring from disappointment, shame, frustration, and anger. They lead from tearful "Why me's?" to cynicism to empty eyes and flat voices that conclude, "It doesn't really matter."

But it *does* matter. Your disappointment matters to the One who created love. God wants our love experiences to be far more fulfilling than what they've been so far. Jesus demonstrated this intent when he went out of his way to meet a woman who had grown disillusioned from her experiences with love. He told his disciples in John 4:4 that he had to go to Samaria, a place "decent" Jewish folk avoided because they felt the people who lived there were beneath them. Samaritans were not kosher (or "pure"). They were a mixed race. The Jews did not agree with their lifestyles or their religious views, so they put a lot of effort into going *around* rather than *through* Samaria. Though Jesus was Jewish, he felt the need to make a stop there. While in the Samaritan desert, after the disciples left in search of food, Jesus sat down by a well to rest and waited until the woman he sought made an appearance.

SO MANY MEN, SO LITTLE JOY

In the previous chapter, we discussed *having no man* and noted that it is easy to believe our happiness and wholeness is attached to something that seems out of our reach. But what if you have what you *think* should make you happy and you still find yourself unfulfilled, unhappy, empty…

Thirsty?

As the story continued, the Samaritan woman Jesus waited for appeared at the well in the heat of the day, and he asked her for a drink of water. Observe that this woman came to the well in the middle of the day. In the desert, no one went to the well at high noon. In the desert, you simply did not do anything at this time of the day. Clearly this woman deliberately timed her visit. She chose to come to the well when she knew no one else would be there, when she could avoid stares of condemnation and whispers behind her back.

You see, she had apparently made quite a name for herself in her pursuit of love, and it wasn't a good one. She must've had something going for her, something that would attract men—looks, charm, that certain way about her. Yet we learn through this story that none of her relationships lasted. We find her alone, subjecting herself to the sweltering heat to avoid disparaging attitudes and comments. How ironic that her desire for love pushed her to take actions that left her lonelier than ever. Stop and think whether any of your relationships have caused you to shut yourself off from people in order to avoid their questions, advice, or disapproval.

Yet there sat Jesus, cool as a cucumber, asking for a drink of water. She was shocked that he would even address her. After all, she was a Samaritan woman; he was a Jewish rabbi. At that time it was also not considered proper etiquette for a man to address a woman who was alone. When you've seen and heard it all and been the target of conversation for as long as she had been, you either break or become bold. So she asked Jesus outright why he had addressed her. Didn't he know he should not be speaking to her? Didn't he know he should not be asking an outcast woman for water, that he would be made unclean by having contact with any- thing she touched? To which Jesus replied, "If you knew who you were talking to and the gift that God had for you, you would have asked *me* for a drink" (see John 4:10).

Many times in Scripture, women are found at a well. Could it be that God intends women to be a source of refreshment to those around them? If so, how can you be refreshing when you have nothing to give? How can you pour out anything of substance to others if you're empty, if the void in your life has never been filled, if you're still waiting for someone to fill you?

The Samaritan woman's response indicates that she seemed to find Jesus' comment ridiculous. After all, she'd heard everything, including an endless stream of lines from the smoothest of men. She decided to put Jesus in his place: "Now why would I ask *you* for a drink? The well is deep and you have nothing to draw water with. And furthermore, how is the water that you have to offer any better than what I've *been* drawing from this well?" She had some deep issues, like some of us. She hadn't met anyone who could reach inside her to the places that hurt. Other men had made promises to her and not fulfilled them. How could this man offer her refreshing water when he seemed ill equipped? What did he have to draw from to fill her need? And how could his offering be any better than what any other man had offered?

But Jesus did not rely on external devices to deal with her internal issues. He didn't require anything to draw from. He *was* the embodiment of all she needed. She could draw her heart's desires from his bottomless well. He knew that his offering could silence the longing of her heart once and for all. He knew that what he had to give could quench her thirst for love. And yet, because he understood that she was disillusioned, he took the time to patiently explain.

SEPARATING THE LIE FROM THE FANTASY

Let's deal with disillusionment and see if we can restore hope to those who have suffered repeat disappointment in affairs of the heart. An illusion is something we see or believe in that is not there or is not true. An illusion is based on deception or a lie. Your heart can create an illusion based on its desire and convince you to believe the illusion—though it is only true in your own mind.

Adam and Eve were seduced by the illusion or lie that they could be whole by themselves—that they could be independent from God, make their own decisions, and thus be like God. In truth, their independence cut them off from God. Adam lost his authority in the Garden. Eve lost the security that came from her dependence on God. Now she would look to Adam to complete and fulfill her, assigning him a job he was not created to perform. Her longing for him to fulfill her would overwhelm and rule over her, causing her deep dissatisfaction to the point of disillusionment. This scenario is true with many women's relationships with men. What starts out as the promise of fulfillment turns into the bitterness of disappointment. With this foundation the woman harbors attitudes and displays actions that are destructive to whatever relationship potential exists. Her response to the man will push him to either distance himself physically and emotionally or to leave entirely. When a woman experiences this cycle over and over, she may shut down her capacity to freely give love.

What's really tragic is that some of us have had the experience of getting what we want and what we thought would make us whole.

After finding out that it really wasn't what we wanted after all, we still cling to it believing that the situation or person will eventually be able to satisfy us. When someone brings up the notion that we can really be satisfied in God, we shrug it off because we still cling to the illusion. Our reaction is like bypassing a cup of water in the desert because we are focused on the mirage of a fountain.

Before disillusionment comes disappointment. To be disappointed is to miss an appointment. You may feel there is a man out there that you'll meet by a specific time and in your heart you have this loosely set appointment. Then you meet a man. In the beginning it feels just like you thought it would, but as the relationship progresses you

THE DADDY THING

Many women have grown up with absent fathers; distant fathers; noncommunicative, nonaffirming, harsh fathers; or even abusive fathers. A father's role in a woman's life is important. But because the importance of a father is overlooked, many men do not take their rightful place in their daughter's life. Dads give girls a sense of identity, belonging, acceptance, and love from a man—before they experience a romantic relationship.

Some women seek the affirmation they needed from their fathers in romantic relationships. Their desire for validation from a man is natural and dates back to the Garden where Adam named Eve and defined who she was. Because many women enter into experience disappointment. You find yourself feeling let down, perhaps even betrayed or deceived. Yet, rather than allowing the disappointment to uncover the lie and clarify that it's not a man who will make you whole, you are prone to think, *Maybe this wasn't the man that will make me whole, but the next one will be.* So you schedule another appointment in your heart and take your brokenness into another relationship where you accumulate more hurts and wounds when that one doesn't work. A cycle begins that lasts for as long as you allow it.

Many of you reading this book can identify with this pattern in your life. The relationship usually starts out great. You throw yourself

relationships with their girlhood needs unresolved, their adult relationships don't work. Their hearts are after something that can only be provided from another source.

Some women find great husbands in spite of this emotional loss. But others reach out unrealistically for love and find hurt. This hurt produces negative character traits such as control, manipulation, insecurity, jealousy, and other unhealthy attitudes not conducive to establishing a healthy love relationship.

On the other hand, many women have good fathers but struggle in relationships to replace their father. The missing link in this whole equation is our *heavenly* Father. Only God can provide the sense of wholeness that not even the best earthly father can give.

into it—heart, soul, mind, and even body. Next thing you know, you are disappointed. You begin to see things that you didn't see at first. The rest is history. Another one bites the dust. You find yourself searching for the remains of your heart among the ruins of yet another failed relationship.

Like the woman at the well you may, in pursuit of wholeness or happiness, have damaged your reputation or felt shame and rejection. It has been said that men love in order to get sex, and women give sex in order to be or feel loved. This may be an overgeneralization, but the statement contains some truth. Most of the time when women get into harmful or destructive relationships, they are simply seeking love based on their need to feel whole, happy, or satisfied.

BREAKING THE CYCLE

Back to our sister by the well. Jesus confronted her with a question, but remember, God's questions are not for information. After all, God knows everything, so his questions serve to provoke us to think, to examine ourselves. Jesus asked the woman to go and get her husband. She told him that she didn't have one. Jesus replied, "That's true. As a matter of fact, you've had five husbands, and the man you're with right now is not yours." Was Jesus trying to condemn her and make her feel bad about where she was? Absolutely not. Jesus declared in the previous chapter, John 3, that his mission was not to condemn but to save us. Yet before we can be whole, we must be delivered from the illusion of what we *thought* would make us whole. Jesus provided her the opportunity to face her delusion by revealing her obstacle to being whole.

What must have been amazing to this woman was that she was conversing with a holy man who, though he knew all this bad information about her, was still interested in her situation. Jesus is also interested in your specific situation. Nothing is too shameful for him to address. He already sees beyond your mistakes to the solution; however, he must first point out the illusion in your life that binds you to repeated disappointment. Our sister at the well carried the illusion that if she could just find the right man she would cease being thirsty. We can probably guess accurately that she didn't want to keep going from man to man but that she was simply searching for the right one. Multiple wrong men later, Jesus, the right man, uncovered the lie.

Remember, your illusion is the thing that you think will bring you the wholeness that only God can give. He must first help you release your illusion before he can make you whole.

In the Garden of Eden where the great disconnect occurred, men and women both received a wound to their heart. The word *integrity* has as its root *integer,* which means whole to a mathematician. An integer is a whole number. When we were disconnected from God, we lost our integrity, or our wholeness, and became fractured. Our disconnect from God severely damaged our identity, and unaffirming life experiences repeatedly deliver the blow. We exacerbate the issue by constantly seeking love relationships that won't fulfill us.

Yet falling in love is only natural because the goal of every life is intimacy. In the Garden God did not want a gardener, he wanted a friend. We are made in his image and crave the same type of deep intimacy and joining together of spirits that Adam and Eve experienced with God before their sin. This is why we spend a lifetime in search of our "soul mate." Our soul mate is really God, and God alone, who breathed the breath of life into us and made us living souls. Our souls long to be joined back to him in an eternal kiss.

This is your true purpose, the root of your very being. It means even more than doing the thing you believe God created you to do. A lot of us are caught up in achieving life goals using our God-given talents, which is important. But if we focus primarily on that, we are not being who God called us to be—his intimate friend. This becomes the "missing piece" we crave.

CLOSING THE LOVE GAP

Consider Romans 14:17 again, that the kingdom of God is not meat and drink, but righteousness, peace, and joy in the Holy Spirit. A sense of righteousness brings with it a sense of belonging and a sense of knowing who you are. It also brings a sense of acceptance. An understanding of righteousness removes the shame that began in the Garden, the thing that causes you to hide, or maintain your distance, from God.

Now that we have established a spiritual basis for fulfillment, please understand that God knows you have natural needs. You can be satisfied in your relationship with God and yet desire to have a mate. This unmet desire, however, should not postpone your happiness. Some people are happy and have no desire for a mate. Obviously this book is not for them. The bottom line is that your desire to have a mate should not hinder you from being a joyful person in God, a person who is full of peace, love, destiny, acceptance, and belonging.

Peace is the absence of conflict—the absence of confusion. The seed bearing this very precious blossom that we would all like to savor is a sense of calm, well-being, and oneness with God. The joy he supplies is at the root of real happiness. Could it be that you are a woman who has yet to drink from the well of God's love for you? Joy is that wonderful feeling that bubbles from being at peace with God and with yourself. Have you allowed the gift of God to spill over from your spirit into your soul and flood your heart with peace, joy, and fulfillment?

There is a feeling that accompanies being in love, which is overwhelming. The feeling is a sense of peace and joy. Your future seems brighter, music sounds better, people seem friendlier. You get the picture; we've all been there. Initially you possess a sense of well-being that can be mistaken for wholeness. A love relationship between a man and a woman stirs us in a deep way and seems to provide our longed-for completeness. The problem is that in our humanity, the feeling cannot be sustained. What was mistaken for wholeness is eventually uncovered as a mirage that merely obscures what can only be imparted to us by God himself.

God does a work of wholeness from within us that cannot be

affected by outward circumstances. The counterfeit feeling of well-being that you might mistake for wholeness comes from a change in your situation, not a change in *you* (what we earlier called transformation). Wholeness is an issue of *becoming,* not an issue of the right circumstances or the right person or the right career move. Some outward stimulus—like falling in love—might temporarily fill you with a sense of wholeness, but true change will not take place without inward transformation. The "high" a woman receives from temporary wholeness in a relationship can lead her to pursue the wrong man, or one relationship after another, in an attempt to recapture that fleeting sense of fulfillment. A form of relational addiction (to that "high") can set in and produce a cycle of unsuccessful relationships.

THE REAL ANSWER

The woman at the well was like the man at the pool of Bethesda. Both the thirsty and the paralyzed were unaware that the solution to their problems was the person right in front of them. Jesus could provide everything they needed and more. In the first story, the proper response to the question "Do you want to be made whole" is a simple yes. In the second story, the proper response to "If you knew the gift of God and who it is that asks you for a drink, you would have *asked* him and he would have given you living water" is a request for that water (John 4:10, emphasis added).

The way to wholeness in both cases was short, direct, and simple.

All the other dialogue between Jesus and this woman and man is about our illusions. Could it be that much of the time we spend with God and with well-meaning friends focuses on obstacles to wholeness versus the source of wholeness himself? Is it possible that being a healthy, happy person is much simpler than we have imagined? What if we would just ask God for the solution and say yes when he offers one?

All we *need* God supplies. A need is something you can't function properly without. Desire is what you want, what you long for. When a desire becomes a need, we are in bondage. It's hard to discern the meaning of desire without understanding need. Need is a survival issue whereas desire is a happiness issue. Needs are always legitimate. Desires can be selfish or irrational. Calling a desire a need falsely legitimizes the desire because we believe that everyone should get what they need.

Once Jesus quenched the Samaritan woman's thirst, she was able to go and talk with the men. That the story uses the words *the men* is interesting. You get the feeling that once her need had been met she was able to offer something to those upon whom she was formerly dependent. Once Jesus made her whole, she was able to see that they were also thirsty. She became the messenger of wholeness to the very source of her past pain!

You cannot have a complete relationship with an incomplete man, and you usually can't recognize his brokenness until you are fixed. Until you are whole, you will find yourself actually attracted to his neediness. You will feel compelled to take on his wholeness as your assignment and then internalize the shame when you fail. Because you *will* fail. The truth is that, when you take on his lack of wholeness, you are superimposing your own brokenness onto him. You are really trying to fix yourself. Instead, your healing must begin with allowing God to free you from your fantasy and change your life from the inside out.

Surely the meaning behind Jesus' gentle words to the love-weary Samaritan woman—"You have had five husbands, and the man you now have is not your husband"—was "Six men and you're still thirsty…" The Samaritan woman came honestly before Jesus and let him shatter her illusions and meet her deepest need. "That's the kind of people the Father is out looking for: those who are simply and honestly *themselves* before him in their worship" (John 4:23, MSG). Being simply and honestly ourselves before God means dispensing with distorted views—and along with them the attitudes of disillusionment and disenchantment that have accumulated as we've pursued what we think will make us whole.

Don't be included among the millions of women who live in the darkness of disappointment, the bitterness of cynicism, and the despair of searching endlessly for a fulfilling relationship. The false notion that the right partner can quench your thirst for love will always produce one man too many in your life. This common form of deception can delay or prevent God from making you whole. Are you still thirsty? Try drinking from the right fountain. It is up to you when the brokenness cycle in your own love life will end.

Things That Make You Go Hmmm...

- Do you continue to date the same man in different sizes, shapes, and colors?

- What need are you trying to fill with that man?

- Do you stay in unfulfilling relationships way too long? Why?

- Do you want a relationship or do you need a relationship?

- How much is your sense of validation tied to having a relationship?

Chapter Three

How Much Do You Cost?

Rule #3: Know Your Value

Once, while on a cruise, I (Michelle) happened upon an incredibly beautiful ring with an unusual stone. It was deep blue with hints of purple when the light hit it a certain way. The jeweler told me that it was a rare gem and that only a few of them with this superior quality were left, as the mines for this particular stone had been closed. He urged me to take advantage of the great deal he was offering. "Trust me," he said. "You will never have the opportunity to get a stone of this quality at this price again! I like you, so I am willing to work with you."

I had no information on the stone other than what the man told me (and I was being cheap), so I passed on it. When I arrived on the next island, there was that precious jewel again—at triple the price. I was sick. I called the first jeweler, but the ring had been sold. He pointed out that the ring had gone for a higher price than the one he offered to me. To this day I still kick myself for not buying it. The stone escalated in value as time went by, and I never saw one as beautiful.

When I finally found a similar ring, exquisite in its own right, I diligently saved my shekels and proudly claimed it on my birthday. As my jeweler handed it to me she said, "Treat it with care. You will never be able to purchase another one at this price." The stone was more expensive than the first, but she was right! The value has now quadrupled.

Due to my ignorance, I initially suffered a loss. Yet I determined not to repeat that mistake when the opportunity arose again. I cherish that ring because I clearly understand its worth, and I will never forget the price I paid for it.

HOW MUCH DO YOU COST?

This should be how a man feels when he has finally captured your heart and made you his own. Women need to understand that the value we place on ourselves has a lot to do with the kind of love we receive.

I (Joel) own a rather expensive four-wheel-drive automobile. When first purchased, it cost a lot of money. It was not the only vehicle to which I was drawn. Several of them appealed to me, but I liked this one the most. The cost of each vehicle prevented me from owning more than one, so this forced me to commit to one at the expense of the others. In order to possess one, I would have to *un*-choose all the others. Deciding carefully was important because the one I chose would be driven for a long time at the loss of all the others. Which one was I not willing to do without?

A man's reluctance to commit may actually be the lack of *necessity* to commit. If the cost of being with you is not high enough, a man might have multiple relationships or, as Aretha Franklin sings it, "a chain of fools." Not everything in life has a price, yet *everything* in life costs. Salvation is free, but it costs you your life. There is a difference between price and cost. Price is a predetermined value set on something being offered for sale. In contrast, cost is determined by the total expense required in emotions and time spent, as well as what it takes financially to obtain and maintain the object of your desire. To think of putting a price on one's love would be to cheapen it. Some things should never be sold. However, a man should have to count the cost to be with you. There is a difference between the price of a marriage license and the *cost* of being married. There is a difference between the price of a car and the *cost* of owning the car. Jesus tells us in Luke 14:28 that before we undertake anything we should count the cost. Usually price is advertised, but *cost* is hidden.

How much does your love cost? How much is your mind, your heart, your soul, and your body worth? You've got to have your mind made up concerning your own value. In case you have no reference point from which to determine your value, let us help you.

Cost prohibits experimentation. Picture this: You are dining in a restaurant, and the waitress says, "We have new rolls, and for today only they are free. Would you like one?" You would probably say yes.

You may or may not be motivated to purchase that roll upon subsequent visits. Suppose the waitress informs you that you could try one of the rolls for ten dollars. You would probably refuse because ten dollars is too much for a taste test.

As a woman, you are not a taste test either. No man should be able to sample you and then decide if he wants to pay the cost associated with claiming you as his own. Neither should he have the freedom to sample and discard you in pursuit of something that he thinks might taste better or have a lower price. You are priceless—fearfully and wonderfully made. God shaped and molded you in your mother's womb. God created you in his own image. You were created, redeemed, and are deeply loved and valued by God. Therefore, the man who wants to be involved with you should have to count the cost.

If being involved with you requires a high cost, you will be able to sift the wrong people out of your life. But having a high cost means you can't be a needy person who always requires the instant gratification of a romantic relationship.

I (Joel) remember shopping at a store in Palm Beach and picking up a belt. The absence of a price tag should've indicated to me that I was in the wrong store. But I asked the salesperson the price of the belt anyway. When she told me the price was four hundred dollars, I knew I could not afford the belt, but I acted as though I was still interested. Being out of my league embarrassed me. Finally I put the belt back on the rack and slowly left the store. While I lingered, the salesperson could have dropped the price to urge me to buy it, but she knew the belt's value. Whether I could pay or not was my business. She didn't change the price to accommodate me. She was willing to forego a sale rather than take less than the value of the belt.

That's the way you have to be. Understand your worth and know your value. Realize that your value does not decrease if you are alone. Your value increases according to your depth of character. Having a man is not what gives you value. Your value was established and stated by God before the beginning of time. "Who can find a virtuous wife? For her worth is far above rubies" (Proverbs 31:10, NKJV). Only you can lower your cost.

Men use women who don't know their value. This happens because women often look to men for validation or affirmation. Sometimes men will try to decrease your sense of self-worth so that they can use you—treat you as an object to be enjoyed and discarded rather than as a person to commit to and cherish.

Losing a relationship can make you feel lost or devalued, but the *man* is the real loser. As that man walks away from you, the thought should haunt him, *I wonder what she would have been like.* He should wonder whether he will ever find someone more to his liking and worry that he may have passed up something valuable.

Have you ever seen two people haggle over price? The person wanting to make the purchase berates the item, even though they want to buy it: "This is wrong with it. That is wrong with it. Here's a scratch. There's a dent. You should drop the price." Once the price is lowered, and the buyer gets the deal, he walks away satisfied and victorious because he feels as though he got a steal. Relationships are similar. When a man is not willing to pay the cost to be with you, he will try to get you to drop your price. He may even haggle with you over your value and say, "Who do you think you are? Mother Teresa or somebody? You are not all *that*. There are other women out there who will if you won't!" He wants you to make yourself available to him, which means lowering your cost. In other words, he wants you to put yourself on sale. And when he can't get what he wants, he'll search for another sale.

COMPARISON SHOPPING

Now, what you must understand is that men are concerned about price. If two men show up at a party in the same suit, they don't feel their uniqueness has been violated, they just want to make sure the other guy paid more for his. Selling yourself short could hinder a possible relationship down the road. Why should someone pay full price for what someone else got on sale?

Women need to realize that an intimate relationship with a man that didn't demand his commitment can cheapen her in the eyes of a future prospect. The new man may hesitate to give a lifelong commitment for something that another person received just for being involved. Quiet as the fact is kept, a man actually feels defrauded by the man who had sex with his wife before he met her. He wonders whether he measures up sexually, whether the man from the previous relationship still has a portion of her heart. He may be uncomfortable with unanswered questions and, as a result, put distance between you.

Past intimacy with another may cause a man to put his heart on reserve. This has been a relationship deal breaker for some.

THE DETERMINATION OF VALUE

How is value determined? I (Joel) purchased a house in 1985, and as of 2002 that house has more than doubled in value. Why? The house has not become a better house—I haven't made any improvements. The intrinsic value of the things inside the house has actually decreased because those items are worn. The essential value of the house is less. So why does it have a higher value than before? Simply because someone *says* that it does.

Value determination is a subjective issue. What worth is to one may not be worth to another. Romans 5:7 indicates that few people would be willing to give up their life for another person, even for the best of us. Romans 8:32 relates that our value is measured by the fact that God did not spare his Son for our redemption. In God's eyes, our value equals the life of his Son.

So it makes sense that God has set the bar very high concerning intimacy and sexual relationships. God determined that lifelong commitment would be the cost of a sexual relationship with you. That is how God sees your value. In Exodus 22:16, God commanded that "if a man seduces a virgin who is not pledged to be married and sleeps with her, he must pay the bride-price, and she shall be his wife." In the Old Testament, there was a cost attached to the privilege of physical intimacy. Today the bride-price remains the same—a lifetime commitment. This is the cost a man should have to evaluate when considering you.

In biblical history a man betrothed to a woman did not get to take her home until he had paid the agreed-upon price for her hand. This may explain why men were often older when they married. Earning enough to afford a wife took time, especially if she came from any notable level of society. Jacob worked seven years for Rachel's hand (Genesis 29:18) and then was deceived into receiving her sister Leah first. So he worked *another* seven years to get Rachel. According to the *New Illustrated Bible Dictionary*, Genesis 29:20 says that Jacob considered the seven years to be a few days to him, so great was his love for Rachel. In other words, when love is real, the cost doesn't seem high. A man who really wants you will do whatever he must to possess your love. So set a standard.

God views every person as valuable because we are all his creation. But what if in the past you have compromised your standards to the point of unhealthy interactions? Didn't I just finish saying that the damaged goods are usually put on sale and sold to anyone willing to take them for a reduced price? Yes, I did, but not in your case! God offers us restoration through his Son, Jesus. We do not have to accept less in the relationship department. Any past failures make you no less deserving of what God intends for you in love.

Knowing your value and God's intentions for you, however, doesn't mean you should demand everything to your exact specifications. There is something to be said for flexibility. For example, when you make a deal with a wholesaler or the like, where there is leeway to bargain, you know ahead of time that any item you consider has already been priced at a 300 percent markup. The standard is set high to facilitate the ritual of bargaining and to make you believe you're getting a good deal. Most merchants who deal this way give and take more or less based on whether they sense the potential for a long and fruitful relationship. They won't mind making less of a profit on your first purchase if they perceive that you'll be a repeat customer. Any loss will be made up when you return. This is the technique utilized in establishing a long-term relationship with a customer. Most smart merchants say, "I want to have a relationship with you, and I want your repeat business. Therefore I will give you this at a price I would not normally offer to anyone else." In the end the merchants reap the benefits of leaving room for a little give and take.

Just as in love there has to be room for give and take. We all know what we would like to receive, yet the reality of what we are given might not be exactly to our specifications. Keep in mind that broadening your options is not the same as lowering your standards. If you know your value, you will recognize when the person you are dealing with has crossed into territory that is nonnegotiable.

What does it mean to broaden your options? Well, knowing your own value means that you will be secure and able to appreciate the value of others. You will know where to give and take in your requirements for a lasting love relationship. A woman might meet a great guy who has all the qualities she has been looking for except that, by her standards, he is not quite there financially. She will be able to judge his character and sense of vision, as well as assess her own strengths and what she will add to him, in order to decide whether she should invest herself in this man. We must maintain balance while holding onto the picture of the perfect love scenario. Many women have married primarily for money and found themselves miserable. No amount of trinkets and possessions can fill a heart that longs for love and affection. Value should never be associated with material possessions. Remember that depth, weight of character, uniqueness (the thing that sets a person apart from all others), and ultimately the cost set by the Creator will determine every man or woman's worth.

Sometimes priceless gems are lost when undiscerning eyes cannot recognize their value. Rumor has it that when Bill Cosby was in college he wanted to marry a young woman whose parents did not like the idea of their daughter marrying a struggling comedian. The rest is history. They obviously missed his other good qualities. I'm sure Camille (the present Mrs. Cosby) would like to thank that woman.

A diamond is merely a rock when first found. Only during the process of refinement are the facets and fire revealed that make it a valuable jewel desired by many and afforded by few. The qualities that determine a diamond's value were present while it was a rough rock. Its color and clarity were already established. A discriminating art lover knows when he's found a rare piece that the world has yet to discover. While others pass over it, he seizes it and celebrates his wisdom as the truth comes to light.

When you know your value, an incredible thing begins to happen—your price shows through subconsciously. The kind of men you attract will begin to change. They will have your same standards and mirror your heart. This does not mean that he will look the way you expected or be what you desired on the surface. But if you hold him up to the light and look closely, you will be able to recognize his value and appreciate his brilliance. And he will do the same for you.

Things That Make You Go Hmmm...

- Have you been selling yourself short in relationships? Why?

- Do you feel as if the man in your life has been getting the better part of the deal?

- What setbacks in relationships have convinced you that your value is diminished?

- In what areas have you discounted yourself and settled for less than you deserved?

- What do you think you deserve?

- How does that affect how others view your value?

What Is Your Name?

Rule #4: Know Who You Are

A name holds weight. The power to name something does as well. This disturbing prophecy, quoted in Isaiah 4:1, seems to be coming to life today:

> In that day seven women will take hold of one man and say, "We will eat our own food and provide our own clothes; only let us be called by your name. Take away our disgrace!"

Where did the man get so much power? Naming is a spiritual concept that has natural ramifications. In the beginning, God gave Adam the authority to name the animals. It was Adam's first assignment in practicing his authority. He had been given the mandate to oversee the operation of God's creation. To be fruitful, multiply, subdue the earth, and have dominion over every living thing was the charge given to Adam and Eve as a couple. God decided that two were needed to carry out this tremendous task. When Adam first set eyes on Eve he declared, "This is now bone of my bones and flesh of my flesh; she shall be called 'woman,' for she was taken out of man" (Genesis 2:23). He gave her not just identity but definition: *You are a separate person in your own right, but because you are a part of me, I will blend your name with mine—wo-man.* He defined who she was. Notice he put her first though he was meant to be her cover—to protect, provide, and lead her in the way that God had instructed him. What he chose to call her did not define who she was or validate her worth; God had already done that. But naming her declared to the world *what she meant to him.* Women today still miss the difference between being affirmed by God and considered by a man. They still attach their value to what they mean to a man. This becomes their identity.

Isn't it interesting to note that when God decided to give Adam a helper he had him name all the animals first? The account goes on to say that Adam named the animals, "but for Adam no suitable helper was found" (see Genesis 2:18-20). Hmm, just because several men parade in front of you doesn't mean any one of them is the right choice. Adam had the good sense to know that none of those animals would work in relationship with him. He was not willing to settle for a hippopotamus or a giraffe, so he rested and allowed God to present him with what was best for him.

Women need to become as discriminating as men are in this regard. Take a clue from Adam. Don't be so hasty to give a man the title of Mr. Right. A lot of women in their exaggerated need for a man have not been discerning. They have settled for dogs and frogs instead of waiting for the man that God calls a good and perfect gift for them.

THE NAME GAME

Each one of us has a specific name so when someone calls us, someone else doesn't answer. A name also means reputation. Cadillac means something different to us than Chevy. The Rolls Royce name communicates something different than Rabbit. All four are names of automobiles and reflect their value. The company that has a strong reputation or a good *name* can demand top dollar for its product because its name has come to imply that the product is reliable, dependable, well made, and long lasting. In the same way, we all have a name, a reputation. That name indicates what people think of us and what we say about ourselves.

If you look into Hebrew, biblical names are typically sentences. For example, Joel means "Jehovah is God." Michelle means "Who is like God." The names given to men and women in the Bible provided those people with a sense of connection to God. Their connection in turn affected the way they thought about themselves, as well as gave them purpose and life direction.

Years ago a psychological study revealed that children who were given made-up names had a higher occurrence of juvenile delinquency. These children had no definition. Most people either mispronounced their names or laughed at them, so the children found themselves having to defend their names and their identities. Because their names were misunderstood, these children often had surly attitudes and rebelled against authority to earn respect. What was initially thought to be an interesting name became a lifetime burden.

The name you are given becomes the spoken definition of who you are, which ultimately affects your life every time someone calls or addresses you. Words have power in the spiritual realm. Proverbs 18:21 says, "The tongue has the power of life and death." What is continually said becomes established. For example, keep saying or confessing, "I'm broke," and see what happens. Your name spiritually establishes who you are. We thank God for creative parents, but when naming children they must be cognizant of what they are creating.

You might be wondering why we're making such a fuss about names, but bear with us. We are laying a foundation. When we enter into a relationship with Jesus Christ and thereby reconnect to God, he renames us in order to redefine our identity. God then calls us more than conquerors, victorious, beloved, new creations. These names were meant to show us how much God values us and to give us specific significance—a personal sense of value and purpose. God, who can only speak the truth, has said some significant things about you.

What do you say about yourself in your own mind and to others? People have knowingly and unknowingly tried to lessen your value since you were born. Some people have astute parents who understand the power of words and say positive, life-building words to their children. But many speak negatively due to their negative nature and the cynicism that is prevalent in our society, even while they hope for positive results. Most people have been battered over time with negative statements made by parents, siblings, teachers, coaches, and even friends. Along the way, you internalized some of these statements until they became a part of you, something you say to yourself: "I never will have anybody… I never will get anything right… Nobody really wants me."

You must allow your heavenly Father to name you. Only he can present an accurate picture of your value. And only he can quiet those negative voices. Several times in the Bible, God used a name change to signify a change in calling, appointment, destiny, and even a change in nature. Abram's name was changed to Abraham, which means "father of many nations," even before he had any children (Genesis 17:4-5). Jacob, which means "supplanter or deceiving one," was changed to "Israel" or "he that prevails," indicating a change in his nature. In the New Testament, God transformed Saul, who was a persecutor of the church, and subsequently changed his name to Paul, which indicated a shift in his calling, function, destiny, and nature (Acts 13:9).

The Bible renames you when you are born again and allows you to see yourself as God sees you. Not only does the Father make you whole in the sense of your well-being, but he also gives you an accurate opinion of yourself—all of which make you feel good about yourself. Every one of us has work to do, and all of us need to change, but God wants to relate to us now. He values you. If God wants you, could you really be that bad?

Even though God gives you a high value, you are the final judge in accepting his view of you. In other words, you know what people say about you, you know what God says about you, But what do *you* say about you? The way you see yourself will determine who you allow into your life and what you expect of them, based on what you know you have a right to.

Allow God to show you just how much you mean to him and to give you the proper self-image. The Bible term for this state of being is *righteousness consciousness.* The root word of *righteousness* is

THE VALUE OF LOVE

Some traditional teaching in the church seems to conflict over this issue of value. No, we do not deserve God's goodness. And we can't earn it. But we are still valuable to him.

When babies are born, the household celebrates them. The nursery is prepared, and relatives come in from out of town. We take pictures and send them to everyone we know. The baby is not performing one duty that has functional value in the home. In fact, the baby is very expensive from a financial, emotional, and time perspective. Even though this addition to the family has not earned our love and attention, there is no disputing the child's value. If we put our faith in Jesus, we are God's children, and there is no disputing our value.

Recognize the difference between value and merit. Value is established worth based on the *inherent* properties of the article. Merit is an earned appraisal or recognition through our own *exter-*

rights, which indicates a sense of belonging, proper standing, or right-standing. An accurate picture to illustrate right-standing with God is as a child approaching a parent. My children approach me (Joel) very differently than their friends or the neighborhood children do. My kids know I provide for them, and I expect them to come to me with confidence, which is another word for faith. The Bible says, "The righteous will live by his faith" (Habakkuk 2:4).

nal efforts to assert our value. The apostle Paul wrote to the church that we are not saved by works but by grace through faith (see Ephesians 2:8-9). It is through faith that we embrace God's grace and receive his promises of a blessed life and eternal security. If value were performance based, then value would vary from one believer to the next. God values us not because of what we've done but because we are here.

Most people have conditions attached to their love: "If you do this then I will love you." If you don't fulfill their needs or desires, they cut you off from their love. This is not true of the one who created us. Earlier we discussed the God-sized void in every person's heart that only God can fill. Associated with this void is every person's need to be loved unconditionally. God's love *is* unconditional. The fact that you exist means that God desired you. He loves you just because you exist. God cannot love you any more and he cannot love you any less than he already does. God *is* love and he loves *you.*

When a child knows who he is and that he belongs, he has confidence and expects his parents to provide for him. In the same way expect God to provide for you. His provision includes the love you need. He is your father. Confidence in God delivers you from neediness. When you have God, you will no longer think you need others to make you whole.

We are the object of God's love, not the cause of it. Why? Because we are his creation formed on purpose with a purpose in mind. He told Jeremiah the prophet, "Before I formed you in the womb I knew you, before you were born, I set you apart; I appointed you as a prophet to the nations" (Jeremiah 1:5). The apostle Paul said that God not only foreknew us, but he also predestined us to be conformed to the image of Christ (see Romans 8:29). Through Christ our love covenant with God is solidified.

The psalmist wrote, "All the days ordained for me were written in your book before one of them came to be. How precious to me are your thoughts, O God! How vast is the sum of them!" (Psalm 139:16-17). Get this into your system. You are not an accident! You are here by divine purpose, and therefore you are loved. Just as we are saved by faith, no works can earn God's love for us. This fact is simply another facet of God's incredible mercy and grace.

YOUR NAME, YOUR POWER BASE

Your name is part of your power base for establishing a love relationship that meets your expectations and desires. Insist that others acknowledge your name or your value. Don't let others call you by a different name than the one God gave you. And don't waste time in an identity crisis if a man has yet to call you by the name you want to hear. The right one will recognize you and address you appropriately. Know who you are, what you are worthy of, and carry yourself in that manner. A man will act with consideration and respect when he knows that you will not tolerate bad behavior.

Once you've settled the issue of what God calls you, and once you are walking in agreement with him, your actions will naturally correspond to your new identity. People will call you or treat you according to their perception of your behavior.

You must first know your own name and begin to introduce yourself correctly. You can't go anywhere without knowing your name. You would be in trouble if you tried to make a reservation at a hotel. When the reservationist asked for your name and you replied, "I don't know," the hotel wouldn't be able to reserve a room for you without a name. A caller wouldn't be able to reach you. If you don't know the name God gave you, then the man God sends into your life will not be able to locate you—let alone know where to place you in his life.

NAMING IT AND CLAIMING IT

When you don't know your name or your value, you may be like the seven women in Isaiah 4:1 who were willing to work for their own keep just to have a man give them a name. Are you working overtime to earn some man's love? Why labor for a man's love when you don't have to work to gain the love of an all-powerful God? If the man in your life is reaping all the benefits of your service but you have yet to enjoy any reward for your efforts, perhaps you've forgotten your name.

When God confronted Eve in the garden about why she had eaten the fruit, she told him, "The serpent hath caused me to forget—and I did eat" (see Genesis 3:13, YLT). She forgot who she was in the eyes of God. She forgot that he lovingly made her and that she had access to all he had. She got fooled into thinking she had to use her own effort to get what she wanted...and lost it all.

Many women have forgotten who they are. They are putting their heart and soul into performing for love and getting no appreciation from their audience. God has a word you can personalize to get you back on track: "No longer will they call you Deserted, or name your land Desolate. But you will be called Hephzibah, and your land Beulah; for the LORD will take delight in you, and your land will be married" (Isaiah 62:4). "They will be called the Holy People, the Redeemed of the LORD; and you will be called Sought After, the City [or woman] No Longer Deserted" (Isaiah 62:12).

When you know your name, you will no longer consider yourself deserted. That's because you will understand that those who didn't care to remain in your life missed out on the opportunity to live in the delightful presence of your love. God enjoys your presence and chose you to be a bride—the bride of Christ. You are already desired and spoken for. God does not intend for you to allow anything less than a godly man to occupy your time.

While you wait for your godly man, you should maintain the posture of a well-kept woman. She doesn't entertain anyone who can't improve the quality of her life—not necessarily financially, but spiritually and emotionally. The person should add to, not take away from, your life. You maintain who you are, and allow God to be picky for you.

God knows both your name and your address. When the right man comes along God will lead him to your door. And that man will recognize your name.

Things That Make You Go Hmmm...

- What have you been subconsciously or consciously calling yourself?

- Does it match God's description of who you are?

- What have other men called you? Do you agree with them?

- What would you like to be called?

- What can you do to help people recognize your true name?

Chapter Five

Does He Want Some*thing* or Some*one*?

Rule #5: Know What He Wants

If you enter any high-end department store you will notice that designer items are not mingled with generic merchandise. They will have an exclusive spot on the floor away from the general traffic, or they have their own floor. That level is usually not as congested as the others. Only those who can afford the prices venture there. (It might seem as if we are using a lot of shopping illustrations, but most women love to shop so we know you are with us.) The analogy describes what it means to be set apart in the right spot in a man's heart. You're the human equivalent to the best designer item, priceless by design, and valuable enough to be set apart.

Women don't understand that men classify women. Men put women in groups—"departments." In his song *Super Freak,* Rick James tells the truth. He starts by saying she was "a very freaky girl," the kind he would not be taking home to his mother. In other words, he was having sex with this girl, but he never intended for his family to meet her or to make a long-term commitment to her. This is an unspoken rule among men. Men classify women, and you need to identify which of the three basic categories you fit in: the freak, the friend, or the forever. You want to focus on being a "forever" and putting your energy only into prospects that are seeking a "forever."

TRUTH

Truth is truth from any source. A prophet is someone who proclaims the truth. Some prophets tell the truth and don't even realize what they're saying. Therefore, listen carefully.

THE THREE F's

Let's first define each category. The *freak* is in a man's life because he's attracted to her, finds her sexy, and gets sexual gratification from her. She may think that because they're having sex, their relationship has the potential for marriage, but he's never even thinking about that. He's simply getting what he wants because she is giving it. He likes her and maybe even feels some love for her. They may have sex together for months, for years. But the moment he meets someone he really values—a woman he's willing to pay the cost for—he will drop the freak and marry the woman he values. To the woman who has been sleeping with him, this can happen in what feels like a shockingly short period of time. He might be married within a few months after meeting the new woman.

Many women are left brokenhearted because they don't understand that they were never in the wife classification—the *forever*—in the first place. Being a forever has nothing to do with how long a man has dated or slept with you but everything to do with how he views you.

The second classification is *friend*. A woman may have a platonic friendship with a man—and that's all it is. Yet women see circumstances differently from men. Women see things a man does not see. Just because you are great friends with a guy does not mean he's planning to marry you. He may be really nice to you, he may say wonderful things about you, he may even tell you that you would be a wonderful wife—all without ever intending to marry you. Friendships with men can confuse women. However, you should still be a friend first. Your relationship should start out as friendship and progress to courtship and then to matrimony. But how can you avoid the situation where the friend you hoped to marry calls you one day and tells you about this wonderful woman he met? He just wanted to call you, his *friend,* to tell you about his happiness.

Learn to listen. Are you foreseeing and imagining a future with someone who hasn't discussed having a future with you? Listen to what the man says. In some cases, men lie and deceive you, but in most cases, women deceive themselves. Men tend to commit to their words. Just because a man is nice to you, friendly, caring, and helpful, don't assume he loves you in a way that will eventually lead to marriage. Protect your heart by really listening to what he says.

Be careful, too, how you imagine yourself with this man. Women often underestimate the power of their imagination. Using their imagination they are able to see themselves in the future. They are able to project their desires onto the wide screen of their life and play out the scenario any way they want. A woman will cast a man into her future the same way a director casts an actor into a play or movie. She will visualize and fantasize a future with this man. She will conduct a relationship with the man all by herself in her own mind. The problem is that when this happens, she has given her heart to the man.

Now don't get us wrong! Anyone who desires to be married and meets someone she is attracted to begins to think about what life would be like with him. But to let these thoughts continue unchecked while she has no promise is dangerous. If you are part of a scenario like this, and your relationship dies before it can blossom into something permanent, you lose. You lose your hope. In your mind, you lose your future. This kind of heartbreak is totally self-inflicted.

You may be saying, "But protecting my heart in this situation is so hard!" Yes, it requires a lot of discipline to be around someone who's wonderful, whom you enjoy, and with whom you think you'd have a wonderful life, and *not* fantasize about what life would be like with him. You must resist those thoughts, though, if he hasn't promised to be in your life. If you don't, you'll find that your disappointment is like a missed appointment. For an appointment to be valid, for a relationship to be committed, two parties must agree upon that appointment. Therefore, to imagine a man in your life without his promise of being there is like making an appointment with yourself. You will most likely be there alone.

God wants to protect you from that heartbreak. In Jeremiah 29:11-13, he says, "For I know the thoughts that I think toward you, says the LORD, thoughts of peace and not of evil, to give you a future and a hope. Then you will call upon Me and go and pray to Me, and I will listen to you. And you will seek Me and find Me, when you search for Me with all your heart" (NKJV). God's work in your life does not change your past, but it can change the effect your past has on your present. If you look to him, his work will help you avoid repeating the mistakes of your past and accept the present for what it is. Right now, in the present, God wants to give you a future and a hope. He does this work by placing hope and desire in your heart. When you allow a man into your heart, you are giving him a stake in your future. Protect your heart: Don't allow a man in without a commitment from him.

How can you tell if you are in the forever category? There are several signs. The most important one is that this man is intentional in his pursuit of you. He does not leave anything to your imagination. He states his intentions for a deeper relationship than friendship. The dynamics of romance and the prospect of marriage begin to surface in your conversations. He invites you to dream with him about the future. His conversation is filled with *us* and *we* instead of *I* and *me*. He begins to market himself as your potential husband by painting a picture of what life would be like with him. You begin to meet the important people in his life. They already know who you are because he has named you to them. He begins to purge activities and people from his life to make more room for you. The rhythm of your relationship intensifies. He seeks out your presence either by phone or in person more frequently and acknowledges when he misses you. There is consistency to his interaction with you. As he becomes concerned with the day-to-day details of your life, more and more of it begins to be integrated into a partnership with his own.

The primary reality to keep in mind here is that you are not assuming anything. Your conclusions are based on words from him that are backed up by actions confirming his intentions. Now that you know how to discern whether you are on his forever list, let's get back to considering whether he should be on yours.

THE WEIGHT OF WORDS

When women talk about a relationship they're in, one they believe is going to end in marriage, they usually respond to the question "What is the man *saying?*" by sharing what he *does*. What he *says* is far more significant. James, one of Jesus' disciples, compares the tongue to a ship's rudder (3:4). The direction of the rudder dictates where the ship will go. If your man is not saying anything about commitment, it means he is not moving in that direction. A sure sign that even a marriage is in trouble is when one or both partners stop saying "I love you." The absence of these words usually indicates that their commitment to each other has degenerated.

You must listen to the man in order to know what his intentions are. The Bible says, "For out of the abundance of the heart the mouth speaks" (Matthew 12:34, NKJV). Whatever he is thinking about is what will be said out loud. If he's sitting around meditating and fantasizing about you being in his life, that's what will come out of his mouth. Hearing these kinds of words from him should be a prerequisite for you to *begin* considering this man for marriage. Notice we said *begin*. After his word has been established, actions must follow.

SETTING YOURSELF APART

As you listen to his words and watch for confirming actions, understand the power of your uniqueness. Establish in your mind that if a man wants some*thing* (sex or a temporary good time), then *any* woman will do. Ah, but there's something awesome that goes on inside a man when he is attracted to a certain woman, the woman he considers his forever. When a man wants *you,* you must be aware that only you will do. This is called the purgative effect of a romantic relationship. If you're the one, other women go by the wayside!

You also possess the power of sexuality, one you should keep an unsolved mystery until marriage. He should wonder what it would be like to possess you completely, until the time he does indeed possess you—on your wedding night. His willingness to wait to fully experience you proves whether he's committed.

Another way to know if you are set apart in his vision is whether he changes his pattern for you. Do you fit into his agenda? Are you a priority? What does he cancel to be with you? (Or what does he cancel *you* for?) Is he consistent with you? Does he remain account-able to you? Does he listen to you? Do your victories excite him? Is he passionate about helping you solve your problems, and does he share his problems with you? Does he respect what you value? Does he respect God? Does sin or a lack of integrity bother him? How does he feel about faithfulness? Is he open to wisdom? What is his vision for his life? These issues are very important when qualifying a man for a potential marriage.

Learn to recognize the intentions of his heart. If you have articu-lated your standards and he opposes your values, then he doesn't value you—and probably never will. Listen to what he's saying, and learn to take what he says at face value. Do you know what his prin-ciples and values are? What is his perception of a relationship? Ask him to give you a picture of an ideal relationship. Then discern whether you fit into that picture.

Most men know that if a woman is attracted to a man, if she feels really great when she's with him, and if she allows him to speak to her heart, she will commit without a commitment from him. She will wait and wait and wait on the man to commit because she does not want to believe that her feelings are somehow not an indication of true love. Now we're back to illusions!

The cheapest player's trick is to call each of his women once a day and say, "Hey baby I was just thinking about you." And that is not a lie. He *was* thinking about all of his women. Thinking that he needed to place those calls if he wanted to keep them. He doesn't have to do anything else to keep them all hoping and wishing and praying for more of him. He balances attention with tension to keep them all exactly where he wants them—willing to do anything to win his full-time affection.

ACTIONS SPEAK LOUDER THAN WORDS

We've emphasized listening to a man's words, but the bottom line is that the words and the actions of your man should add up. Interview him early in the game. Does he want to get married one day? Have children? Where does he see his life going in five years? What does it look like? What does it include?

While you're asking the questions, make sure you don't attach your desires to them. If he tells you that marriage is not in his immediate plans but later down the road, believe him. You will not change his mind. Men decide when it is time for them to get married and *then* search for a mate. In other words, they decide they need a wife and then they search for someone who is qualified to fill the bill. Women, on the other hand, fall in love and base their decision to marry on how they feel. Men do not. If he does not ask you to have an exclusive relationship with him, assume that you are not in one. Consider and enjoy your other options. Do not behave as if you are in a committed relationship when you are not. Doing so will only entangle your heart and set you up for disappointment and heartbreak. If he doesn't tell you he wants to be in a committed relationship, consider yourself officially "just a friend." How many times have you or a friend been told those famous last words by a man as he dove into a serious relationship with someone else: "But I told you we were just friends!"

Now, if a man *has* asked you to commit to a serious relationship with him, yet you see red flags, ask him (nicely) why. Let's say his calling pattern and quality time spent with you are inconsistent, and maybe there are periods of time when you don't have the slightest idea where he is or who he is with. Ask him why, and listen to his reply. If he gives you a nebulous answer, something or someone else is in the picture, perhaps some unfinished business. He will never admit this to you if he is in the process of weighing his next move. He will try to float both options until he makes a decision. Help him decide. Remove yourself from his options. The saying, "You never miss the water 'til the well runs dry," applies here.

Make up your mind that the man in your life will be faced with a decision when he meets you, because he is not meeting the average woman. You, like the designer articles we mentioned earlier, have been set apart from the masses. Your uniqueness carries a high price. You will not be put on sale. Full price is the only price that is acceptable to get your attention and love.

Therefore, pay close attention to the customer. Listen to him. Is he just looking? Or is he ready to buy? A good shopper knows that paying more for higher quality makes the purchase a long-term investment. God made the initial investment into you. The man in your life should add to that account.

Things That Make You Go Hmmm...

- What are you saying about your relationship with the man in your life?

- What is he saying? Do his words indicate where you stand in his life? If so, what are they and where do you stand?

- Which category (freak, friend, or forever) do you currently fall into?

- Have you met the family and close friends of the man in your life?

- Are you in a relationship whose definition is unclear to you?

- Do the actions of the man in your life imply love and commitment, or is he just a nice guy? What signs form the basis of your conclusion?

Chapter Six

Protect Your Heart

Rule #6: Keep Your Heart in the Right Place

On a trip once, I (Michelle) switched purses for an event and inadvertently left my wallet on the bed at the hotel. Halfway to the venue I discovered my oversight, so I immediately had the driver take me back to retrieve it. I got back to the hotel, hurried to my room, breathlessly scooped up my wallet, checked its contents, and sighed a relieved thank-you to the Lord. Everything was intact.

I didn't have some huge amount of money in the purse—quite to the contrary—but my driver's license, my insurance cards, and my credit cards were in there. One little pouch seemed to contain my entire life! My identification, my protection, and my ability to provide for myself. You never realize how valuable your driver's license is until you've lost it. Without it you can't prove your identity. Credit cards, though they can be hazardous to the average person's budget, are valuable too. You can't buy a house or a car without established credit. I couldn't afford for someone to take these things.

In most cases when a thief swipes someone's purse, he rummages through it for money, jewelry he can pawn, and credit cards to use for a quick shopping spree. Then the thief throws the purse and its remaining contents into a garbage can near the scene of the crime. So most women are very cognizant of where they leave their purses. They don't set them down and walk away in a crowded place. They hold them close to their bodies when walking down a congested street. They are protecting what is valuable to them.

Women should be even more careful with their hearts.

Until this point, we have established that you must understand your value, know your name, and know how to set yourself apart from other objects of desire. Now we have to discuss protecting your valuables, because you don't leave valuable things around for the taking. The way we protect valuables from the uncaring and the undiscerning is by limiting their accessibility.

And there is nothing more worthy of protection, nothing more precious, than a woman's heart. Your heart condition affects every area of your life and can be the death of you if mishandled. How your heart feels affects your sense of identity and determines your self worth. Women are created with a deep capacity to love. Therefore you must be careful. You cannot afford to throw your heart to the wind and hope someone catches it. We are encouraged not to cast our pearls before swine (see Matthew 7:6). That verse doesn't mean men are pigs. But it does mean that if a man doesn't recognize the value of your love, he will do the same thing with your heart that pigs do to pearls in their sty—trample them underfoot and crush them into the mud.

Not only should the man's motive toward you be checked, but your motive toward him should be checked too. Why do you want this man? Though your heart is valuable, God considers his heart just as valuable. Therefore, consider if you are willing to *give* what you

THE DIFFERENCE BETWEEN LOVE AND LUST

Love is the desire to benefit another even at the expense of yourself: "For God so loved the world that He gave…" (John 3:16). Selflessness is the ultimate indication of whether a man is loving you from a pure place. The emotional opposite of love is hate; the spiritual opposite is fear; but the moral opposite is lust. Understanding the difference between love and lust will help you discern a man's motive for being in your life. Here are some comparisons:

LOVE	LUST
Love gives.	Lust takes.
Love is easily satisfied.	Lust is never satisfied.
Love grows.	Lust dies.
Love is patient.	Lust rushes.
Love serves.	Lust demands.
Love appreciates.	Lust depreciates.

desire to receive. And make sure that his heart toward you is filled with pure intentions.

To learn how to discern intentions, let's take a deeper look at the heart. Proverbs 20:27 says, "The spirit of man is the lamp of the LORD, searching all the inner depths of his heart" (NKJV). E. W. Kenyon, in his book, *The Hidden Man of the Heart,* says the subconscious is the spirit-man. When the Bible talks about the heart, it is not referring to the blood pump, it is referring to our inner man. Scientists say that we consciously operate at only 10 to 12 percent of our mental capacity and that the rest is our spirit or subconscious. We can therefore conclude that we operate consciously at about 10 percent and subconsciously at about 90 percent.

HEART CONDITIONS

In Jeremiah 17:9-10, we are told that "the heart is deceitful above all things, and desperately wicked; who can know it? I, the LORD, search the heart, I test the mind, even to give every man according to his ways, according to the fruit of his doings" (NKJV). Let's break that down and see why God would make such a statement about what seems to be the most tender spot in our being. The word *wick* means braided, woven, or twisted fibers. The word *wicker* describes something made of twisted cane or straw. The phrase *a wicked heart* is a twisted heart, a heart that seeks answers from the wrong source. God also describes the heart as being deceitful. James 1 states that it is possible to deceive yourself, so let's clarify the meaning of deception.

Deception is to believe what is not true, to trust what will not stand up or perform as promised. So this verse is saying that your heart has the capacity to set its hope upon something that will eventually result in disappointment.

Jeremiah also said, "Cursed is the man [or woman] who trusts in man and makes flesh his strength, whose heart departs from the LORD. For he shall be like a shrub in the desert, and shall not see when good comes, but shall inhabit the parched places in the wilderness, in a salt land which is not inhabited" (17:5-6, NKJV). Clearly you will be frustrated if you look to people for answers. If you set your heart upon people, you "shall not see when good comes." Earlier in this book we talked about having tunnel vision to the point of being blinded to other things. Focusing on the wrong source for your needs can actually blind you to an answered prayer. In other words, what you want is there, but because you are looking so hard at something else, you don't see it. If your attention is in the wrong place, you could miss the person that God sends your way.

On the other hand, "Blessed is the man who trusts in the LORD, and whose hope is the LORD. For he shall be like a tree planted by the waters, which spreads out its roots by the river, and will not fear when heat comes; But its leaf will be green, and will not be anxious in the year of drought, nor will cease from yielding fruit" (17:7-8, NKJV). The woman who sets her heart upon God and plants herself firmly in God's Word will always be fruitful. Her happiness will not be seasonal; she won't just be up when everything is going right and down when everything is going wrong. She has another source of joy, another source of power that lies deep and undisturbed beneath the environment and away from volatile circumstances.

When you choose to live your life in the spirit, you will find consistency. When you are spiritually minded and spiritually ruled, you won't go through the ups and downs of people who trust in their environment. Yes, you will have problems and seasons of trials, but they won't affect your peace and your joy.

God wants us to turn our hearts back to him as the source for everything. God uses many channels to bless us, but he wants to be the source. Proverbs 3:5 says, "Trust in the LORD with all your heart, and lean not on your own understanding" (NKJV). It is possible to be sincere, yet wrong. Verse 6 says, "In all your ways acknowledge Him, and He shall direct your paths." Sensitivity to God is very important when it comes to matters of the heart.

It has been written and said that your heart makes a decision and then your mind rationalizes it. In other words, in matters of the heart or matters of relationships, our decisions don't always make sense. The biggest mistake women make is that they give their hearts too quickly. What they don't realize is that once a man has their heart, he has their mind. If a man has your mind he has you. He has broken your strength. You will be weak for him and open to all of his manipulations. No wonder God in-structed us to love *him* first with all of our heart, soul, mind, and strength. He didn't want you to leave any part of yourself open to mistreatment. If you give your heart to God, he will protect it. This is what it means to be "hidden" in God (see Colossians 3:3).

MUSIC TO YOUR EARS

The way a man wins your heart is not with style, not with his looks, but with words. A man is moved by what he sees; a woman is moved by what she hears. One of the chief ways of protecting your heart is by watching what you allow a man to say to you. "Group dating" can be your insurance to help protect you from needless injury. Interesting aspects of a man are revealed when you observe him functioning in a group. You have a chance to see if he's trying to win your attention, or if he likes everyone's attention; if he is caught up in drawing women to him, or if he really desires to be in your presence. A sincere man speaks from his heart with sincerity to draw you into a mutually beneficial romantic relationship. An insincere man has practiced and mastered the art of speaking directly to a woman's heart while his heart remains disconnected. His goal is not to be committed but to get what he wants from you. In other words, you need to recognize that the wrong man can say all the right things.

Old King Solomon said in Proverbs 30:18-19 that "there are three things which are too wonderful for me, yes four which I do not understand: The way of an eagle in the air, the way of a serpent on a rock, the way of a ship in the midst of the sea, and the way of a man with a virgin" (NKJV). How does an eagle stay aloft? How does a serpent not slide off a smooth surface? How does a ship not sink? Why does a man cling to something he cannot master or control? All of these defy logic, just as a woman's actions do when she gives a man access to her heart. She becomes irrational.

LOVE WHO LOVES YOU

How many times have you seen a woman constantly give a man another chance when the man has already proven who he really is? She has given him her heart. Women tend to love men they love, rather than love men who love them. The writer of Proverbs referred to wisdom in a feminine context, because there are characteristics of wisdom that should be characteristics of women: "I love those who love me, and those who seek me diligently will find me" (Proverbs 8:17, NKJV). In other words, wisdom will never pursue you but will demand to be pursued. Wisdom knows her value. She knows she will produce favor in your life, so she expects to be pursued and appreciated. All women should follow her lead.

Leah married Jacob, as described in the book of Genesis, but he did not choose her. Jacob loved and wanted her sister, Rachel. He was willing to do whatever he had to do in order to attain Rachel's hand. So even though Leah had a husband, she struggled with feeling unloved. Her work to gain Jacob's love was never enough because she hadn't been chosen. In other words, you can have a man, but if you don't have his heart and his desire, you will find yourself still feeling alone.

Pursuit is the evidence of someone's desire. One of the worst words of advice the world gives women these days is that they should pursue men—that they should just go after the man they want. Women don't realize this is a setup for them to be put down. Taking this posture places a woman in a very vulnerable position. If you are pursuing a man, what is his cost? He doesn't have to move out of his normal pattern or his normal rhythm to have you in his life. So how can you know what value he places on you? Remember that anybody will eat the free roll because it doesn't cost anything to experiment with it.

Pursuing a man is an open invitation for him to experiment with you without cost. The Bible says, "He who finds a wife finds a good thing, and obtains favor from the LORD" (Proverbs 18:22, NKJV). This verse puts the man in the pursuing role. His position as pursuer is important because pursuit forces commitment. If a man isn't willing to pursue, he probably isn't willing to commit. You may have a wonderful relationship with him at first, and the man may even celebrate you, but the fact that he doesn't value you enough to pursue you means that your relationship probably won't last. If the relationship does last, the burden to initiate romance, and the advancement of the relationship, will remain on you. Once you give away your heart, getting it back is difficult and painful.

Here's an example: Let's say you're in a room, and there are two guys present. One knocks your socks off, and the other one is just okay. If the guy who is okay is the one pursuing you, you'll probably talk to him. But all the while you will still be hoping the other guy, the one you are *really* attracted to, will talk to you. Now should the one you are *really* attracted to come your way, you will probably drop the one who was pursuing faster than he could finish his last sentence.

That's what makes you vulnerable as a woman when you pursue a man. You don't know whether or not a man really wants you, and this feeling sets you up for insecurity. If you get a man through your pursuit, you will never feel secure because you did the picking. What if he decides to pick someone else? On the other hand, if the man chooses you, whenever you have an insecure moment, you have the memory of his pursuit to silence your fears. We can confidently love Christ because the Bible says that he first loved us. He chose us and pursued us.

Now, some women are impatient and would rather not take the time to find out if a man really wants them. They just want a man. Remember the woman at the well? Her problem was not the fact that she couldn't get a man; her problem was that she couldn't get a man who made her *whole*. A man should desire you. Proof of desire is pursuit. If he is not pursuing you, he doesn't want you.

Keep in mind that just mildly wanting you is not good enough. His level of willingness to pursue you might indicate something deeper in him. Perhaps he's just shy. Or perhaps he's been deeply hurt in the past and has trouble trusting women. You may think, *Perhaps I should give him a call just to check on him. He might have lost my number.* You know all the excuses. None of them hold water. Whatever his reason, if he's not pursuing, beware. If a man does not have enough aggression in his nature to pursue, he will likely be passive across the board—in pursuing success and in caring for his home and his family. Even though you got the man, you will eventually lose respect for him when you feel the entire household load falling on your shoulders.

Let's play out another scenario and say that the man is indeed aggressive in other areas of his life. His actions should be an even clearer signal to you that he is not the right man. If he can pursue other things but doesn't choose you or pursue you, he might like you, but he doesn't like you enough. He still has someone else in mind. He is still searching. When he sees her he will know she is it and pursue her.

But don't date a man *solely* because he is in pursuit of you. Pursuit alone does not qualify a man to be in your life, but if he doesn't pursue you, he doesn't qualify for your consideration. If you are too easy, most men are smart enough to sense that you may be too easy with others. They will begin to doubt your integrity and your moral character.

Cheap may attract, but quality lasts. When a man is looking for a mate, he's looking for something that will last. Make sure that you are in a love relationship where you are celebrated and not simply tolerated. The way to insure your position is to allow yourself to be pursued and won. Every man celebrates winning. Let your love be a trophy he displays proudly.

Things That Make You Go Hmmm...

- Does he call you, or do you call him?

- Who initiates each phase of the relationship?

- Does it seem important to him to impress other women even when he is with you?

- Does he ask for more of your time than he gets, or does he get more of your time than he asks for?

- Are you insecure when you haven't heard from him?

Chapter Seven

The Issue of Attraction

Rule #7: Recognize the Invisible Man

I (Michelle) have a friend (who shall remain nameless or she might kill me) who longed for a mate for years. When she prayed about it, she would always ask the Lord to give her a man like her first true love. She and that first love had broken up ages before, and both married other people. They hadn't seen each other in years, yet she fondly remembered their relationship and attributed its failure to her own immaturity at the time. Well. Not only did the Lord fulfill her prayer, but he also went one step further and gave her back her first love!

One day my friend received a call from her first love. He told her he had been trying to find her for quite some time. Both of them were single again and had been for years. She had since become a Christian, and now he was a believer too. They were married last fall. When I asked her how married life was after waiting and praying for so long, she told me the most profound thing I have ever heard a married person say about his or her mate. She said with tears in her eyes, "I can't believe how happy I am. He is not a perfect man by any means, but he loves me the way I've always wanted to be loved. I feel as if God is loving me through him, because what he does is not humanly possible." She went on to say how he anticipated her needs and seemed able to feel her heart.

After I heard that, you could have knocked me over with a feather. I walked away pondering what she said. The depth of her words went to my very core. I found myself reconsidering my own wish list for Mr. Right. Truly I had experienced men in my own life who had loved me deeply, yet not one was what I had in mind for myself. Had I sacrificed the love she described due to what might have been superficial considerations? After all, we all want someone finer, richer, stronger, funnier… Shall I go on? The fact of the matter is, there will *always* be someone finer, richer, stronger, funnier…whatever. But the question is will they want you? Will they have the capacity to love you the way you want to be loved?

OUTWARD ATTRACTION

Let's talk about what you desire in a mate, especially with regard to attraction. When you feel attracted to someone, you are not dealing with the core aspects of the person, because the inner attributes are not what you first observe. (Please know that this book is not going to tell you to marry someone who is a good person inwardly but repels you outwardly. You should be attracted to the person you marry. We do not believe God's will for your life is that you marry someone who doesn't attract you outwardly. God loves you. He wants you to be able to love and celebrate the person you choose to spend the rest of your life with.)

Your views on what is attractive, depending on how long you've been single, may change over time. But let's start with where you are currently. Take time now to make an attraction list, and be honest about it. What type of men attract you? What features are important to you? Looks, style, mannerisms, dress? Are you attracted to men with money, with education, with status, with a sense of humor, with a sense of adventure? When Christian women talk about what they want in a mate, the first thing they usually say is "I want a Christian mate." This desire is a good thing, but Christian singles in most churches have a difficult time finding a partner. They have trouble because there is an attraction crisis in the church, even in churches filled with singles.

The problem is that many (not all, of course) Christian women find Christian men to be boring. The traits that have been promoted and emphasized to men in churches are good and necessary for stability and security. They are character traits. Being faithful, dutiful, honest, and having integrity are desirable qualities—but they aren't exciting. All women want these characteristics in a mate, but these are not what initially *attract* you to a man. You will never hear a group of women comment on a man who has just entered the room with "Ooh girl, check him out! He's so faithful, so full of integrity, so honest! My, my, my, his heart is the bomb!" Mmm hmm. You are looking at something else when a man walks into the room, whether or not you are sanctified. Clearly there is a problem here. Yes, your old nature was crucified when you accepted Christ, but your personality remains. And Christians should be themselves. Unfortunately, many become cookie-cutter believers, imitating what they think Christians should be like. Trying to do this will get you in trouble and make you a very boring person.

THE IMPORTANCE OF CHARACTER

Now we're talking about personality. There is a difference between character and personality. The Bible says much about character and little about personality because God has predetermined that everyone's personality should be different. He delights in our uniqueness. Be true to your personality. If you are a naturally humorous person, you should not try to become a quiet, serious person. Doing that would be incongruent to the way you were created. On the other hand, if you happen to be the quiet, serious type, you should leave the funny stuff to someone else.

Clearly personality is important to attraction, more important than physical attraction, but personality alone fails to tell us enough about the inward person to make an informed decision. The elements of attraction (such as appearance and personality) that are important when we first meet someone will not be as important as the information we find out later. I (Joel) have friends telling me all the time about women they would like me to meet. The first thing I think about—but the last thing I ask—is how does she look? I don't want to appear carnal, shallow, or immature, but this really is the first thought that comes to mind. I'm still growing in this area, but I do understand that, though attraction is important, the features that initially attract me to a woman are the least important in qualifying her for marriage.

Remember our root issue is wholeness. Lack of wholeness can cause us to be attracted to a person for the wrong reasons. If you don't know who you are, and you're looking for someone to complete you, you will be looking for features in him that you lack yourself or for qualities that you feel will give you validation with others. For example, you may desire someone really good looking, not because you are especially attracted to him, but because being on his arm wins you acceptance. In other words, you're telling yourself that you must be okay if this good-looking man wants you. (Perhaps this is why women sometimes beg physically attractive men not to leave them. If the man leaves, the woman thinks her value is walking out the door.) You may be overly attracted to men with means if you have struggled financially. Or you may fix your attraction on someone whose occupation would give you instant status—like a politician, a famous person, or a successful pastor—if your destiny seems vague. Looks, money, and power can be attractive, but with God as your provider, you don't need a husband for those things.

Even your own neediness can push you to be attracted to someone whom, under normal circumstances, you wouldn't give the time of day. If you haven't eaten for a while, a cracker can have the appeal of filet mignon, so don't be fooled by attractions while you are in a needy state.

All these deficiencies in people can play into attraction, so we need to have a strong sense of who we are. Proverbs 27:7 says that "honey seems tasteless to a person who is full, but even bitter food tastes sweet to the hungry" (NLT). The same verse can apply to married people too. A married man who is satisfied may find a woman attractive without feeling attracted to her because he is already fulfilled with his wife.

Look now at your list of attractions. You will notice that you could have everything on that list and still be unhappy. The impression we have of a person in the early stages of meeting him does not give us enough information to consider that person for the long haul. There is another picture that we need to be concerned with, and that is the person's character. When we study the etymology of the word *character,* we find that it means "picture" or "image." The person's character is the photograph of the inward person. Man is a spirit, has a soul, and lives in a body. The spirit and the soul make up the inner man, the real person.

When you have known a person for a long time, you really don't see their appearance as much as you see the real person. Think about a person in your life who is a really good person. When you think about him, you think about his characteristics. He is faithful, loyal, a person you can depend on, and a person who has come through for you when you really needed him. Although he may not be overly attractive on the outside, you think of him fondly. We can take this a step further and infer that, as your affection for him grew, he began to appear more and more attractive to you.

On the other hand, there may have been a person in your life who was attractive on the outside but turned on you. He may have deceived you, betrayed you, and let you down. He may have ultimately ended up being a bad person for you. When you think of this person, you don't see a beautiful person. You see an ugly person because the photograph you now have is of the inward person, the one you had to deal with, not the one you originally saw.

Learn how to identify good character. Proverbs 31 will help because it describes a certain virtuous woman. The author praises her attributes while never mentioning her looks, and he concludes his tribute to her in part by saying, "Charm is deceptive, and beauty is fleeting; but a woman who fears the LORD is to be praised" (31:30). So if a woman (or a man) fears the Lord, she will be a person of great character with wonderful, desirable attributes. Galatians 5:22-23 gives us another photograph of good character: "But the fruit of the Spirit is love, joy, peace, patience, kindness, goodness, faithfulness, gentleness, and self-control."

What is going on inside a person is the most important factor when you consider marrying someone. You do not marry the outward person; you marry the inward man. If he has a bad character, your chances of being happy with him are slim to none. Faithfulness is the cornerstone of character. Marrying someone without character means at the least that you can't count on him. Ask yourself, too, whether the person is a loving person. One of the worst things you can ever do is marry a selfish person. Imagine submitting to someone who puts you last. And does the person have his own source of joy, or do you constantly have to cheer him up, pump him up, and encourage him? When we talked about disappointment earlier in the book, it had to do with setting an appointment by yourself. If you set an appointment with a person of bad character, you schedule yourself a disappointment.

Some women have what we call a "broken chooser." They choose based upon attraction and overlook the inward picture. Disrespect, disloyalty, laziness, inconsistency, and impatience are ignored because of her attraction to a man. Your chooser must be adjusted so that you do not focus on the aspects that attract you to the person. You must not allow what your heart and hormones feel to override what your mind sees and comprehends of the person's character.

CHECK OUT HIS VALUES

While you examine his character, you need to examine his values. Opposites attract but similarities remain. Remember in the Garden of Eden, God created couples, animals as well as humans, after "like kind." There was a reason for this. The Bible asks how two can walk together unless they agree (see Amos 3:3). It also states that if two are in harmony concerning anything they ask for, they will have it (see Matthew 18:19-20). Further, God had to break up the group of people trying to build the tower of Babel because he said, " 'If as one people speaking the same language they have begun to do this, then nothing they plan to do will be impossible for them. Come, let us go down and confuse their language so they will not understand each other.' So the LORD scattered them from there over all the earth, and they stopped building the city" (Genesis 11:6-8). The place of power in any relationship is the place of agreement. Much can be accomplished when two agree. Marriages based on common values therefore have more potential to last and a greater capacity for effectiveness than unions born out of a strong attraction between people who are opposites.

Keep in mind that there is a huge difference between attraction and respect. You can actually be attracted to someone you don't respect. For an extreme example of this, let's examine a guy at a topless bar. He sits in trancelike awe of the woman dancing in front of him. Should his daughter, sister, or mother come out to dance, however, he would be enraged. This man does not respect the woman on the platform. He is merely attracted to her. Lack of respect can cause great pain and eventually kill a relationship. When you are emotionally healthy, you will have a deep attraction to someone you deeply respect because you both share the same values. Shared values are necessary for a happy and long-lasting relationship.

When considering a mate, listen to his values, his priorities. If your values don't match, decision-making in your home will be tough. One of you will probably be disappointed in many decisions because, based on your own values, you would've made a choice in each case different from your spouse. For example, if you are the kind of person who values saving money and this is your top priority, and the other person values buying whatever he wants, you will have problems. If one of you is a conservative and the other a liberal, there will be constant disagreements. If one of you is highly social and the other is extremely introverted, there will be many moments of loneliness. At first these differences may seem cute, interesting, and even exciting. You may convince yourself that this person is good for you because he will balance you out. But over time, value differences will wear on you. It is important to have the same values. That both parties are Christians is just the door opener.

As a Christian you should not even consider marrying someone who is not a believer. The Bible addresses this in 2 Corinthians 6:14 (NKJV). The term is *unequally yoked.* In the same way, a nonbeliever should be with someone who agrees with their spiritual persuasion. There are other important areas that should be equally yoked in relationships: passion for God, views on relationships, giving, politics, money, how to raise children, standards of living, how men and women relate, the role of the man, the role of the woman, and so on. Whether you are equally yoked in these areas is very important in considering a lifelong mate.

So values need to be shared *before* you give someone your heart. It is awful to give someone your heart and then find out that deep down you don't respect him or agree with him on the important issues in life. Perhaps this is why the subject of submission is such a heated one. Allowing someone to lead you is difficult when you don't like where they are going. Many women in the courtship phase do not scrutinize a man's ability to solve problems or make decisions. After exchanging vows, she then decides he is not qualified to do so. She begins to take the lead because she does not trust her husband with the details of their lives, which frustrates him and forces him to abdicate other responsibilities. All the while deep in the heart of a woman is a silent cry, *I wish I could find a man who could take care of me.* And yet most women do not trust the man in their lives to take care of them because they do not respect his character and values. Find out ahead of time if you will feel comfortable allowing the man you are considering as your life partner to be responsible for your life. Ask yourself this question based on what you now know about your man: "If I fell into a coma for a month, when I woke up, would everything concerning my life be in shambles, or would it be in order?"

CLARIFY YOUR VISION

Are your visions complementary? Does he have a vision? Marrying a man without a vision is dangerous because you don't know where he is going. Joining your life to that mystery—or should we say misery—may mean signing up for more adventure than you would like! Know where he is headed because you may not want to go there.

If the dream and desire of his heart is to minister the gospel to the indigenous people in South America, and you're the kind of person who wears high heels to a picnic, he may not be the right guy for you. If it's your dream to minister the gospel in the wilderness, and his desire is to live in a high-rise in Manhattan, you're going to have a problem. Knowing his vision is very important because, as a woman with biblical values, God expects you to join yourself to your husband's vision. It will be to *your* advantage if your visions complement one another.

Be patient and get in touch with what you really want because "what the righteous desire will be granted" (Proverbs 10:24). And Proverbs 13:12 says, "Hope deferred makes the heart sick, but a longing fulfilled is a tree of life." Later, verse 19 says, "A longing fulfilled is sweet to the soul." That's a whole lot of talk about desire. All desires obviously are not good; therefore, you must be able to distinguish between the desires of the flesh, the mind, and the heart. Check the motivation behind your desires to determine if they are godly.

Once you become a whole person, you will be able to get in touch with what you really want out of marriage. Knowing what kind of marriage you want means you have a vision. If you already know, you need to write down those features. Habakkuk 2:2 says "Write down the revelation and make it plain on tablets so that a herald may run with it." Once your vision is on paper, it will be established in your mind and you will be tied to it. It is difficult to stray from a standard once you've established it clearly.

In her book, *The Path,* Lori Beth Jones talks about a woman who wrote down what she wanted (her vision) in marriage. Her list seemed unreasonable at the time. After reading it, you would think, *This man does not exist!* For example, she wanted someone who would be prosperous yet who would be home to greet her when she got there. She made out her list, and three years later she met a man who had been a builder and was very wealthy. He had grown weary of traveling and wanted to stay home. She received her dream.

Vision determines your path. If you don't know where you're going, it doesn't matter what road you take. My (Michelle) book *If Men Are Like Buses, Then How Do I Catch One?* explains that if you want to get on the right bus, the first order of business is to find out if that bus is going in the direction you want to go. Knowing where you're going determines the path that you take. In the same way, if you don't know what kind of husband you want, any guy will do. But once you have a vision and a strong sense of what kind of marriage you want, write it down and visit it often. That way you will keep fresh in your mind the things that qualify a man to be a potential candidate.

Lori Beth Jones also says there are three things that having a vision does in your life: (1) It causes you to sift through possible candidates, (2) it helps you set boundaries, and (3) it serves as a magnet. With a vision, you will be able to separate the eligible from the ineligible, as well as make informed decisions on how much access you give each person to your life and to your heart. You won't waste your time dating someone you are not considering for marriage. You won't take a chance on giving your heart to someone who doesn't qualify for your vision of marriage.

Your vision will also help you set boundaries concerning where you will and will not go. Women often cross boundaries they shouldn't cross—not because they don't know that they're doing wrong but because they have no vision. Sad but true, "where there is no vision, the people are unrestrained" (Proverbs 29:18, NASB). The real reason for discipline is vision, but discipline without passion is legalism or religious activity that will wear you out. In other words, if your discipline for staying on point is not accompanied by passion for your vision, you will find yourself bottoming out emotionally and forfeiting your long-range vision to settle for short-term gratification.

Finally, vision serves as a magnet. Have you ever purchased a car and suddenly you see that car everywhere? You didn't know so many people were driving the same type of car until you purchased yours! This is how we see selectively. Jesus said, "Blessed are those who hunger and thirst for righteousness, for they will be filled" (Matthew 5:6). This is a spiritual law: what you are hungry for, you attract. You will also attract what you are at your very core. Realizing this can be a bitter pill to swallow if you do not like what you have been attracting. Those who believe strongly in commitment have no time for commitment-phobics. And those who sense your vision stay away if they don't share it. The kind of man you *want* will be attracted to the kind of woman you *are*.

One warning: What and whom you are attracted to can be a reaction to a recently failed relationship. A bad experience with a man who possesses a certain quality or characteristic can cause you to be temporarily attracted to an opposite characteristic. For example, because of the conflict in a past relationship, you may be attracted to a man because he's very quiet and peaceful. If this aspect of him isn't what you really want, you may ultimately find him boring, and have another failed relationship on your hands. So watch the decisions you make as they relate to the season of life you are in. To do this you must become quiet before God. Take the time to get healed of past hurts so that you are free to make objective and rational decisions concerning what you truly want from a man and from your relationships. Sometimes it is better to be by yourself while you allow your mind to clear the dust from your recent emotional upheavals. Then and only then will you be able to view the object of your attraction clearly.

In sum, make sure that what attracts you is in agreement with your values and is able to fulfill your long-term needs. Like a high-priced item in a boutique, a costly piece could be attractive but not practical. It might look good, but it won't wear well. Some men appear attractive but can't go the distance in a relationship. Don't get distracted by your needs when considering characteristics that attract you. Never make a decision that will have long-lasting effects under the duress of a temporary need for relief or change. And finally, allow your decisions to be driven only by what you know about yourself and what is good for you in the long run.

The second half of Proverbs 29:18 says, "Blessed is he [or she] who keeps the law." Obedience to God's Word, as well as to your principles, guarantees you will get the results you want.

Things That Make You Go Hmmm...

- What do you want in a man?

- Describe a time when you acted on strong outward attraction and ignored core differences in a relationship. What was the result? How will you avoid doing this in the future?

- What does the picture of your marriage look like?

- Are you involved with someone who could make your picture come alive?

- If yes, how is this picture different from your past relationships? If you answered no, that this person does not make your picture come alive, explain why. What makes you stay in the relationship?

Chapter Eight

Desire vs. Need

Rule #8: Know What You Want

Have you ever wandered through a store and found yourself staring at an article of clothing that you just loved? You knew you didn't *need* it, but you *wanted* it. If you managed to walk away, the article probably haunted you; that is, until you looked at the other five things you had at home that resembled it. But if you were swayed by your desire and purchased the item, you might have experienced a twinge of guilt over being self-indulgent, then kept it anyway. Or, you might have had such a bad attack of buyer's remorse that you eventually returned it. There are lots of things we *want* in life, but we don't really *need* them.

Perhaps you *do* need that item but not right now. Desire presses you to have it immediately, whether or not it is in your budget. That's when we all get into trouble. We convince ourselves that we won't be happy until we get that thing. Yet God wants us to be content in whatever state we find ourselves (see Philippians 4:11). Bottom line? There is nothing we should feel we can't live without except God.

In Genesis 29, we learn that Leah was married to a man who didn't love her. She wanted his love; she felt she needed it. Her way of trying to get his attention was to have children. After the birth of each son she would say something like, "Surely my husband will love me now…" or "At last my husband will become attached to me…" But with the birth of her fourth son, she realized her ability to give her husband sons had no bearing on his heart toward her. She stopped performing for the love of a man and turned her affections toward the only One who she knew would return them. She said, "This time I will praise the Lord." In the time it's taking for a husband to come your way, perhaps God is trying to get you to understand that he must be your first love in order to guarantee you happiness in any human love that follows. He wants your heart to be planted safe and secure in good soil, not open to the elements that could destroy it.

THE WILDERNESS EXPERIENCE

God will allow us to go through seasons of drought in order to redirect our attention back to desiring the right things. He did this to the Israelites in the wilderness. Moses said in Deuteronomy 8:3, "He humbled you, causing you to hunger and then feeding you with manna, which neither you nor your fathers had known, to teach you that man does not live on bread alone but on every word that comes from the mouth of the LORD."

Notice especially the phrase "man does not live on bread alone." The Word of God is the bread of heaven, and because you are a spiritual woman as well as a physical person, you need spiritual food as well as physical food. Yet there is something deeper here. God took the Israelites through the wilderness so that they would know they don't live by bread alone but by every word that comes from the mouth of God. Food represents much more than simple nourishment. Most of the time we don't eat what we *need* to eat; we eat what we *want* to eat. A news program recently said that 63 percent of Americans are overweight. This situation did not come from an overindulgence of oat bran, millet, and lentils. It came from people attempting to find satisfaction through what they eat.

Most people scour the menu at a restaurant not for the most nutritious item or what packs the most vitamins but for what most closely matches the taste they have at that moment. The children of Israel did not rebel in the wilderness because the manna was not nourishing. It might have been the most nutritious food in the history of mankind. They rebelled because they didn't like the way it tasted. What are your tastes? Are your tastes healthy or are they unhealthy? What do we really want out of a relationship?

Religion does us a disservice when it teaches us to kill our desires. A misunderstanding of the flesh and the spirit often implies that we must kill everything that seems fleshly. But you are not supposed to kill your desires; you are supposed to master them by bringing your mind, will, emotions, and body under the control of the Holy Spirit and thus by living a spirit-led life.

THE SOURCE OF DESIRE

Because all desire is not good, we must examine and locate the sources of our desire. We quoted the Bible earlier as saying the desire of the righteous shall be granted. And Mark 11:24 says, "Therefore I tell you, whatever you ask for in prayer, believe that you have received it, and it will be yours." On the other hand, on the subject of needs the Bible advises to take no thought for your life because your Father knows what you need before you ask him (see Matthew 6:25-34). The Bible talks a lot more about being happy than it does about survival. Ideally, the believer is supposed to live on earth with his needs met, petitioning God only for his desires.

Often singles end up feeling guilty because of their deep longing for a mate. Married people exhort them by saying something like, "You have God in your life—that should make you happy," or even by quoting a scripture such as "Seek first his kingdom…" (Matthew 6:33). We have to be mindful that the Bible says seek *first*, not *only*. It is perfectly legitimate for a single woman to have a deep longing for a mate and family. God made her that way. The problem arises when this longing distracts a woman to the point of robbing her of her joy. A joyful life is the result only of wise choices and purposeful living.

But how can you make right choices if you don't understand

your own motives? Most wrong decisions are rooted in selfishness or fear, based on what you feel you need at any given moment. James taught that it is possible for us to pray to God with wrong motives (see James 4:3). Motive and intention are subtle but powerful drivers in our lives. Hebrews 4:12 teaches us that the Word of God is able to reveal motives and intentions of our heart. Many people, because of wrong motives, are working the wrong job, living in the wrong city, and possibly even married to the wrong person. Many people live at survival level and reach merely for safety rather than destiny. If you are living one life and desiring another, take the cue. Let God use your desires to lead you into your purpose. Allowing God to sort out your motives and desires will help you make wise choices in love. Why? Because your decisions will be motivated by your sense of purpose. Purpose brings great fulfillment and joy, which is your ultimate heart desire. Marriage does not change your purpose. Your purpose should become the compass that directs all the decisions of your heart, so you're asking yourself about each marriage candidate, *Will this person add to or subtract from my purpose?*

Perhaps you don't know what your purpose is. How will you find out? One way to know your purpose and reason for being is to ask yourself this question: *If I could do anything I wanted and get paid for it, what would I do? What would I do for free?* Your purpose will ultimately be your highest passion. In his love for us, God has united pleasure and purpose. If we are going to live in the will of God, his primary way of leading us is by the desires of our heart.

CLEANSING YOUR PALATE

As with the children of Israel, God will lead us through wilderness seasons to change our taste, to change our desires. Sometimes you are not in touch with what you really want until what you thought you wanted is removed from your life for a season. I (Joel) recently finished a forty-day fast in which I eliminated sweets from my diet. I had always really liked sweets, but it wasn't until the fast that I realized I had developed a need for them. When a desire becomes a need, we are in bondage. I was in bondage to sugar. It would talk to me. It would make demands on me. Sugar had become a god to me. It was during this wilderness time of fasting from sugar that God changed my taste and set me free from its bondage. Without even exercising, I immediately began to lose weight and to feel healthier because I had taken the false god out of my life.

After gazing at some old photographs of myself, I (Michelle) asked God to give me back the body I used to have. God said that if I would give him my body for three months and do as he said, he would do just that. His instructions were simple: Do a Daniel fast. I was only to eat fresh fruits and vegetables and drink only water. I was to eliminate all sugar, fat, carbs, and dairy from my diet. No rice (help me, Jesus), no potatoes, and no bread (my other big addiction). I thought I would never be able to do it for that period of time. But I found myself able to stick with it no matter what anyone presented to me. I was even able to pass up my dad's fried turkey wings. Now that was supernatural!

As my energy level soared and the weight fell off, I found that I no longer craved the things I thought it would be impossible for me to give up. I truly did not miss them. Once I came off my rigid diet, I found I could no longer eat the way I did before. My appetite had changed, and since then I have been able to maintain a healthier approach to eating. What I previously thought I needed to satisfy my palate, I no longer desire.

All this brings us back to our original issue of wholeness. When you are not whole, it is difficult to distinguish between desire and need. A person may start out wanting sex. When they become addicted, they need sex. Many people, even people in the church, cannot imagine how people can be celibate. Their desire for sex has been replaced by a need for sex. It has become a god to them and can even get them to disobey God's laws. Remember: Real pleasure does not come from getting your *needs* met, but it does come from getting your *desires* met. When a desire becomes a need, it's no longer a matter of pleasure, it's a matter of survival. Smokers continue to smoke because it becomes normal to them to do so, even if they no longer enjoy it. The same can be said of any sin. People continue to sin because it feels normal, even if they are overwhelmed with guilt. Bondage becomes normal. And people forget what freedom feels like.

Sometimes we declare that a desire is a need to justify and honor it. I've heard some women say, "I need a man. I need to be with someone. I can't stand being alone. I need a husband." You don't *need* a mate. Single people thrive. They enjoy themselves and their freedom while maximizing the advantages of being single. They are happy and fulfilled people. You've got two witnesses here. Happiness is a wholeness issue. If you want to be happy, you need to be whole. If you want to be married, you simply need a mate. If you want to be *happily* married, you need to be a whole person married to *another* whole person.

There are two great dangers in marrying out of need. First of all, you will not be marrying out of genuine desire. Second, because no man can make you whole, whatever you are searching for won't be found. A marriage born out of need will eventually become a disappointment. Talk to the Holy Spirit about your perceived needs and allow him to adjust them. You may need to be without a person in your life during this time. This is what we mean when we refer to the wilderness. Wilderness time allows God to make you whole. He begins by stripping everything away and cleansing your palate. He then adjusts your tastes by bringing your desires into alignment with what is really good for you. Once your needs are met in God, you will then have a more accurate view of your desires.

GET A TASTE ADJUSTMENT

I (Michelle) was always attracted to the wrong type of men. So I declared a man-fast for a season of my life to adjust my taste in men. After being alone for a time, I woke up one day startled at the full realization that I had not keeled over and died while manless! As a matter of fact, I was a pretty happy camper. Actually happier than I had been for quite some time. So when I ventured back out of my self-imposed shell, I was protective of my happiness. I was quick to eliminate anyone I felt would threaten my newfound peace of mind and contentment. As time went by, I was surprised to note that I now attracted a different type of man altogether. These were good men, desirable men, men with good intentions. Hmm. Things were getting interesting. I know what you're thinking, but don't ask. I'm taking my time deciding.

The point is, when you change, your desires change. As we discussed in the previous chapter, what you desire, you tend to draw. This is why certain types of people seem to find each other with little effort. Even in church it only takes two or three Sundays for the intercessors to hook up with other intercessors, worshipers with worshipers, complainers with complainers. People are like walking magnets. The same is true with your destiny. For example, when someone makes a decision to start a certain business, she begins to run into people who can assist her or who know someone who can. How many times have you heard new converts say, "As soon as I decided to change my life, I began to bump into Christians"? So it is in relationships. When you weed out the desires of your heart that were rooted in wrong motives, you get in sync with your destiny and aspects of your life accelerate—including relationship issues.

Organize your thinking and get a clear vision of your needs and desires. You will have to pray in order to discern your desires. Begin by searching your heart as you examine the vision you wrote down in the previous chapter. Visit it often. Even if you don't want to box yourself in by listing traits that have to do with looks and profession, there should at least some nonnegotiable desires that you refuse to stray from. For instance if you are a Christian, your first nonnegotiable should be that he must be a believer who has a committed relationship with Christ. Faithful, honest, loving, and having a sense of vision should be other nonnegotiables at the top of your list.

As I was prayerfully considering a man in my life, I (Michelle) had a very telling dream. In it, this man and I were in separate cars heading toward a destination that he had selected. Somehow, as we drove, I ended up in front of him. I kept looking in my rearview mirror to check with him to make sure I was going in the right direction. After a while I said to myself, "Wait a minute! Why am I in front of him? He should be leading. After all, he is the one who is supposed to know where we're going." I pulled over and allowed him to take the lead. Shortly thereafter I realized we were lost.

The dream helped me take another look at the man in my life and realize that he didn't know where he was going. I couldn't help him get wherever it was he thought he wanted to go because he himself wasn't clear on his destination. To unite myself with this person would lead to a life of uncertainty for me. I would be lost. There was the possibility that I would lose sight of my own God-given goals as I became distracted trying to help this man move forward. As I considered other moves this man had made in life, the evidence showed that he had no concrete vision and was not open to sound counsel—a bad combination. He was still searching to find himself, while I have an extremely clear vision of my purpose. To align myself with him in a marriage would take me off course. I politely took him out of my mate consideration file and placed him in the friendship file.

Revisit your list of desires and divide your list into two columns: Negotiable and Nonnegotiable. This will help you come up with a more realistic list and give you some room for give and take. Perhaps there are some things you can do without on your want list, but definitely do not stray from your nonnegotiable list.

Remember that God has promised to give you what you need. As a matter of fact, he already knows what you need, including the things you haven't realized yet. This is why it is important to trust him through the wilderness while holding onto this certainty: After God has revealed the true issues you need to deal with and recalibrated your heart, he will lead you to the Promised Land, and you will be able to recognize it.

Things That Make You Go Hmmm...

- Have you labeled a desire as a need to elevate its importance?

- Have you allowed God to adjust your desires to be in agreement with what he desires for you?

- Can you distinguish between desire and need?

- What motivates your choices?

- Do you know your purpose?

- Is God trying to give you a taste adjustment? What will it take to let him?

The Force of Patience

Rule #9: Be Patient

Everything we've talked about up to this point takes time. It has been said that patience is the weapon that forces deception to reveal itself. It is the insurance against being deceived or making wrong decisions. Some things can only be made known by waiting. God takes his time. After all, he has eternity. And he is detail oriented. Details take time. We want to wait on God, spend intimate time in his presence, and discern his heart for us.

The only way to receive what God has for you is by waiting. Patience was one of the differences between the first king of Israel, Saul, and the more legendary, David. Saul was unable to wait as Samuel, the prophet of God, had instructed him, so he moved ahead of his instructions and began to offer sacrifices to God himself. He was a king, yes, but he was not a priest. This was not his calling (see 1 Samuel 15:22-24). He had not been ordained by God to offer sacrifices. Saul's impatience caused him to get out of place. Those who have control issues take matters into their own hands in haste when they feel that God is taking too long to bring about the desired conclusion to their situation. Samuel told Saul that God had rejected him as king and was seeking someone who was after God's own heart—in other words, someone who would wait, someone who had sound enough character to trust in God and not fear people. Saul's acting on impatience and impulsively taking control cost him everything.

THE WORK OF PATIENCE

Waiting can be tough in relationships with men as well, especially when you feel you've finally found the one you've been searching for all your life. However, we are instructed to "wait on the LORD [and] be of good courage" (Psalm 27:14, NKJV). Be confident that God is able to keep circumstances concerning you under control and reserved for you. If that man is yours, he will still be there when the time is right. Love is not like a last call sale. It's not as though love will be gone if you don't make a move now. Put things on hold until you are absolutely certain that this is the best choice for you. The wrong decision can cost you too much.

Anyone can maintain a facade for a certain length of time, but patience is a revealer. If you wait, patterns of consistency and inconsistency will eventually surface. People do things in patterns. Without patience, you don't have the vantage point to observe his patterns in other relationships, as well as in life in general. Are his friendships short term or long term? Is he excited about you, or is he is excited because you are the new one in his life right now? Is he in love with love, rather than in love with you? Some go to extremes to create romantic moments, but when the romance fizzles, they move on. They move from moment to moment, collecting wonderful experiences, but they never commit.

How does he handle money? What is his track record at work? Is he always in transition, or is there constancy in his life? Is he a person who makes impulsive decisions, or does he seek, obtain, and act on wise counsel? Does he own up to his mistakes, or is he always a victim? Some patterns take longer than others to surface. With careful listening to him and listening to those who know him, the truth will surface. Patience allows you to get down to root issues and protect your heart.

We talked in an earlier chapter about the need for good character in the man you might marry. Now let's talk about your character. Patience is a character issue. Some jokingly say, "I'm just impatient," as if it is a personality trait. But impatience is not a personality trait; it's a character flaw. Patience is a part of the fruit of the Spirit, and God expects you to develop it (see Galatians 5:22). The Bible says love is patient.

Isn't it interesting that when you fall in love, patience is *not* one of the things you feel? That's because *falling in love* and *love* are two different issues. Falling in love is about how I *feel*. Love is what I *do* for others. Remember Jacob's tireless patience in working a total of fourteen years to win Rachel's hand? When it's love, waiting won't seem long or unreasonable.

One of the ways patience is developed is by not giving in to pressure. Exercising your will against the pressure to react to a situation increases your ability to act wisely.

UNDER THE MAGNIFYING GLASS

The ability to wait and be patient says a lot about you. It says you are whole, secure, your needs are met; and you are protected by this ability. A person who is not patient is vulnerable. The Bible says a man (or woman) who cannot control his spirit is like a city with broken down walls, unprotected (see Proverbs 25:28). When you meet someone you are attracted to, the impulse is to run into a relationship and experience all of the good feelings. Reigning yourself in, while taking time to examine things more closely, will take character.

Have you ever seen an item you wanted to buy, and something told you to watch and wait, but you purchased it anyway? Then a week went by, and you discovered it was on sale. If only you had waited, you could have saved yourself needless expense. Too many women marry someone and soon say that the man flipped on them overnight and became a completely different person. The pain they experience is very real, as they wonder where they went wrong. But they must take responsibility for the choice they made. When these women are asked to recount their relationship from the beginning, the red flags become glaringly obvious. They were in such a hurry to marry, they didn't examine their mate as closely as they should have.

I (Michelle) knew a woman who had a crush on a man for many

years. Finally he gave her the time of day and, after dating her for two weeks, asked her to marry him. She purchased rings for *both* of them. She planned an elaborate wedding overseas and got her friends caught up in the excitement. I get breathless just recalling the events. This man paid for *nothing*. This woman drained her savings. No one could convince her to slow down. The romance blew up on the honeymoon night. They never lived as a married couple. The money she had poured into him and her wedding was gone and caused her financial hardship for some time. She later commented that I was frowning in every wedding picture. Small wonder, I was still stuck on the fact that he had not even had enough money to purchase her engagement ring. How was he going to take care of her? What was she thinking?

Lack of patience is a major flaw in the lives of many women. They give their hearts as well as their bodies much too soon. Yes, even church girls fall in their race to reach the altar. Let's revisit the word *integrity*. One of the ways the term *integrity* is used is in relationship to bridges. If a bridge can hold up under pressure, it is said to have integrity. Can you hold up under pressure? Do you have integrity? You probably never thought of rushing into a relationship as a lack of integrity. Luke 21:19 says, "By your patience possess your souls" (NKJV). Patience is what maintains you as the master of your soul. If patience is a fruit of the Spirit, it stands to reason that impatience is a tool of the Enemy.

Patience expresses our freedom to obey God, but we don't like to do that because obedience usually means we have to suffer a little longer for all the pieces to fall into the right place. If you really trust God, then you can't do without his divine timing and his attention to every little detail for your life.

You might be ready, but that man might not be ready. Perhaps God is putting the finishing touches on him to present you with a good and perfect gift: "So do not throw away your confidence; it will be richly rewarded. You need to persevere so that when you have done the will of God, you will receive what he has promised. For in just a very little while, 'He who is coming will come and will not delay'" (Hebrews 10:35-37).

THE POWER OF CHOICE

Choice is a powerful dynamic in your life. When choosing, you are the master of your choice. After choosing, you are the servant of it. Thirty seconds of rage can get you twenty years in prison. Running one red light can leave you disabled. One night of casual sex can leave you with a child to raise alone or with a disease that ravages your body. Choices we made under the pressure of a man's advances or our own needs and desires can lead to awful consequences.

Let's say you've met a great guy. You're dating. Everything is feeling good. Sunshine is brighter, food tastes better, people don't seem as bad as they usually are. Even rainy days are beautiful. This just might be the one. Good, we're happy for you...but wait right there. Hold steady. Hold on to your principles. Keep your heart locked up for a while longer. Keep your body to yourself. It might seem like agony to not follow your feelings, but God has promised that he, "after you have suffered a little while, will himself restore you and make you strong, firm and steadfast" (1 Peter 5:10). Standing on principle will get you all that you long for—if you can hold out for the prize. If your man can make it through the waiting period, he is a serious contender. Remember that this is your power time. You are the master of this choice. Should you choose to marry him, you will have to serve that choice. Stay steady and do the reality check.

READY OR NOT

What are we checking? First, does he love you enough to protect your jewels—your heart and your body? A woman's power base in a relationship is her uniqueness, her sexuality, and her mystery. Your ability to wait will set you apart. Men can smell desperation a mile away. It causes them to either flee or take advantage. On the other hand, when they sense that you are not in a hurry, out of intrigue they draw closer. Your mystery comes into play here. Don't be so quick to let a man know *every*thing about you too soon. Give him something to long for, something to discover. You should be like a treasure box, offering new little surprises every day. Keep it interesting. When someone tells you the end of a movie, how do you react? You no longer want to see it. They ruined it for you. So maintain your mystery.

As a child, when you discovered your Christmas presents before the holiday, it took the fun out of unwrapping them on Christmas

Day. Why give the most precious gift you have—your body—to a man prematurely? As P. B. Wilson says in her book, *Knight in Shining Armor,* God designed men in such a way that they will commit if women will be patient and maintain their sexual purity. Every seventy-two hours, testosterone hits a man's system. It is his wake-up call to find a wife. When a woman gives her body before she has a commitment, she's put the man back to sleep. He doesn't have to wake up; she's given him a sedative.

Recently Rutgers University issued the results of a study on why men are taking so long to commit to marriage. The number one reason was that sex is too readily available without having to make a commitment. The second reason was because men could enjoy the benefits of marriage in a live-in situation and did not feel the need to marry. When a woman gives a man her body without the benefit of marriage, she has stepped off her power base. If you insist on doing this in pursuit of a lasting relationship, you are a volunteer for disappointment.

In 2 Samuel 13 you will find the story of Amnon, King David's son. He was obsessed with his half-sister Tamar to the point of illness. He fancied himself deeply in love with her, and the longing for her overwhelmed him to the point of depression. So, with a little help from a crafty cousin, he cooked up a scheme to have his way with her. He pretended to be ill and convinced his father to allow Tamar to come to his room, cook for him, and serve him a meal. So Tamar came to tend her ailing brother in all innocence. But upon her arrival, Amnon ordered all of the servants out of the room and raped her. Tamar protested and begged that he ask his father, King David, for her hand in marriage, but he couldn't wait. After the deed was done, the Bible says he hated her more than he had loved her. How quickly things changed.

Poor Tamar was used, discarded, and disgraced. She was considered undesirable because she had been violated. But the story doesn't end there. Her brother Absalom seethed for years because of what his brother Amnon had done. Not only was he angry with Amnon, but he was also angry with his father, King David, for doing nothing about it. (David had also had his round with impatience when he stole Bathsheba from her husband Uriah. So perhaps he didn't feel qualified to speak on the matter.)

In the end, one act of impatience cost several lives. Absalom finally took revenge and killed Amnon. He continued to seethe until he later rebelled against his own father and tried to steal the kingdom. The captain of his father's army finally struck him down. This story clearly shows us that the consequences of impatience are more far-reaching than one can possibly foresee.

A man must be willing to wait to have you completely. If he lacks control now, what will he do when you are ill or off on a visit to your mother? Dating is not for mating; it is for collecting data. Your patience in maintaining your integrity will reveal whether this person even qualifies for *courtship,* let alone *marriage.* What is he made of, and what are his intentions toward you?

LOVE AT FIRST SIGHT

A man I (Michelle) know told me that after taking his wife out to lunch on their very first date, he knew he would marry her. After the date, he immediately went to a jeweler, selected a ring, and began to make payments. He did not, however, ask her to marry him for four months. He observed her during that time to make sure he had made the right choice. She maintained her purity throughout their courtship, and when he could wait no longer, he popped the question.

A man knows what he wants to do with you, but you can change his mind through your own impatience. Do not grow weary of well-doing or maintaining a standard of purity, "for at the proper time we will reap a harvest if we do not give up" (Galatians 6:9). What you withhold will purge him of any reservations he may have about losing his freedom, fears of committing, and the voices of dissent from his friends who don't want to lose a comrade to marriage.

When Ruth went home to tell Naomi about her discussion with Boaz about the prospect of marriage, Naomi advised her to wait (see 3:16-18). Naomi was sure that Boaz would not rest until he had set everything in order to win Ruth's hand. Boaz had uttered a silent intention in his heart concerning Ruth from the beginning. From the moment he saw her, he was moved to protect and provide for her. As she bided her time, those feelings had room to grow. By the time she broached the subject of needing a man to redeem her, he had already arrived at his intention. There was nothing left to do but fulfill it. (Though we will discuss Ruth's experience in more detail, we suggest you read her entire story in the book of Ruth.)

A key principle in the kingdom is sowing and reaping. There are several factors that can cut off your harvest. Luke 8:15 says that if the ground is good and not compromised, the harvest is reaped with patience. This implies that impatience could cost you your harvest. How many people have had the desire of their heart and the answer to their prayers for a lifelong, loving marriage within reach and blew it by trying to harvest it before it was ripe? Mark 4:28-29 says that the seed is sown and the harvest comes in stages, first the blade, then the ear, then the full corn in the ear. Only then does the farmer put the sickle in and reap the fruit of it.

How does this apply to you in natural terms? The seed of attraction is sown in the man's heart. The blade is his initial interest. He then gives you his ear; he listens to your heart. In his pursuit he seeks to fill your heart with himself, and this takes time. Then the corn comes into its own. The farmer can't force it. But when true love is ripe, it is easily plucked for the enjoying. As the Shulammite woman said, "Do not arouse or awaken love until it so desires" (Song of Songs 8:4).

There are many forces at work when you fall in love. Patience allows love (the desire to benefit another at your own expense) to become the preeminent force in the relationship. Love is going to hold the relationship together; not infatuation, attraction, or even desire. Love will allow a couple to endure the hard times—sickness, unemployment, problems with children, old age, weight gain, pregnancy, temptation—all those things we fear will threaten our long-term relationship. Love is worth waiting for.

I (Michelle) have just recently learned a powerful lesson about the virtues of patience. I have felt the pressure to "grow up" and buy a home for several years but have never been able to press past my inner reservations. To those around me, my owning a home was becoming as pressing as getting married. My friends were relentless in expressing their frustration about my reluctance to make this major move. Why hadn't I done it yet? They were beginning to make me think something was wrong with me! I prayed about it, and God told me to wait. Well, that just didn't make sense to me, so I would go looking anyway at new developments and open houses, but nothing felt quite right. "Wait," the Holy Spirit would quietly say each time. I questioned God about why I should wait. Weren't my friends right? Wasn't I being irresponsible? Think of the tax benefits, Lord! Again, just a quiet urging to wait.

One day recently, I acquiesced to a realtor friend who suggested we just go looking for the sake of gaining education about the market. Feeling no pressure, I went. That's when I found the perfect place! I had given my friend my list of criteria and my budget limitations. He had already told me that I would never find what I was looking for in the neighborhood I wanted for the price I quoted. He said I was being unrealistic. After we had finished the negotiations for the place I selected, his comment was, "Girl, God likes you! You got everything you wanted, the neighborhood you wanted, *and* within your budget! Unbelievable!" We later discovered that the unit I purchased originally had been listed for $200,000 more than what I paid for it! God in his omnipotence knew about the upcoming blow to the economy. He knew that interests rates were going to be at an all-time low, and he told me to wait so that I could have everything I wanted at a price I could afford. I thought of those who had rushed to buy before me and were all scrambling to refinance. Truly impatience costs. But here is the moral of the story: If God can be so specific about giving me the real-estate desires of my heart, can't he do the same thing with a man? How much more specific will he be? How much more does he want to protect my heart and make sure that love doesn't cost me my self-esteem or even my faith? Think about it ladies, and be willing to wait on the Lord.

Things That Make You Go Hmmm...

- Are you feeling an urgency to close the deal in your relationship?

- What are you afraid that you will lose if you wait?

- How does he respond to you setting the pace in the relationship?

- What do his actions indicate to you?

- Are there any red flags about this man that you have been ignoring?

Magical Thinking

Rule #10: Be Realistic

A princess walked beside a pond one day and encountered a frog who said that if she kissed him he could turn into a prince. The princess, being quite familiar with fairy tales, promptly kissed the frog. When she opened her eyes, she discovered that he was still a frog! "I thought you were supposed to turn into a prince!" she exclaimed. The frog smiled. "I only said I *could*. I didn't say I *would*. Ribbit!"

Promises, promises... And so it goes with many of us.

What you *think* and what *is* are two different things. Women must live *in reality*. We tend to fall in love based on how a person makes us feel. Remember the heart makes the decision and then the mind rationalizes it. So before you turn your mind over to your heart, look at your situation without coloring it by how you feel. That is living *in reality*.

Do not become involved in an emotionally intimate relationship with anyone that you wouldn't want to marry. You can, but then you'll need my other book, *Prayer Guide for the Brokenhearted*. A woman once told me (Michelle) that she wrote her list of must-haves, and when she met men, she sized them up against her list. If they did not match the description, she stopped seeing them. Her rationale was, you can fall in love just as easily with a man who is not right for you as one who is. A safeguard against falling in love with the wrong man is not allowing him to occupy valuable space in your life. For a long-term goal to be realized, it demands your immediate discipline. We need to take a sober look at several issues before we give our heart away.

Do your homework. Learn about his past relationships. How did those other relationships end? Were they painful, bitter exchanges? Was every relationship like a soap opera? What is his parting view and description of the other person? Remember that even though he tells you that she was crazy, he chose her. What does that say about him? Remember it takes two to tango, so never just readily take his side. There are always three sides to every story: his side, her side, and God's point of view. Prayerfully ask God to reveal this man to you. Check out his friends. If you don't like his friends, something is wrong. You might say he is not like his friends, but we beg to differ with you. He is simply not like them when he is around *you*. Birds of a feather flock together. It's just a matter of time before you see which direction they are flying.

The sad truth is that most people don't change, although all of us need to. Has there always been drama in his life like a revolving door of relationships and jobs? Reality is that probably won't change. Except that you will be added to the mix. Therefore, when considering this man, our question is not what's *possible* in this relationship, but what is *probable*. Based on his character, what is this man likely to do? Hopefully you are going to grow as your life progresses, and growth naturally involves change. Your partner should grow with you. A willingness to change is a characteristic that should be high on the list you have for a mate.

Women often make the mistake of thinking that they can change the man after they are married. But the best time to observe change is *before* you are in a committed relationship, because the man at that point is highly motivated to win you. You have powerful leverage at this stage, when he desires you but doesn't have you. If he won't change to win you, then he surely won't change after he has you. Moffatt's translation of Proverbs 16:26 says, "A laborer's appetite labors for him; his hunger drives him to work." You don't have the power or the authority to change a man, but his desire for you can drive him to make the changes necessary to qualify himself for you. For example: You can always tell when a teenage boy meets a girl he likes. You smell his cologne from twenty feet away. His shirt is tucked in (well maybe it's just pressed). He cleaned his tennis shoes. Whatever! The bottom line is that his patterns have changed because he is trying to win someone.

The one responsible for changing us is the Holy Spirit, and if that's your name, then you surely have no use for this book.

A MAN'S GOT TO DO WHAT A MAN'S GOT TO DO

When a man wants something, he is motivated to get it. This is generally true for everybody. *Again, unrequited desire forms a purgative affect in an uncommitted, nonsexual relationship between two people who are attracted to each other.* The desire to win you, if it is present, will begin to weed out all desires your man has that are not conducive to winning your affections. If you settled for your man "as is" and went ahead and married him, insistence on change at this point could cause conflicts, indifference, or abandonment.

The tension created by a man wanting you but not having you, as a single woman, will force him to think through the cost of being the man in your life. He may decide that you are too expensive, that you are not worthy of his changing. Committing to him too early takes the pressure off of him. If you do that, you will be stuck in a tough relationship or faced with a painful breakup.

One way that a man knows he has you is when you make yourself too available. If you give him all of your time, he knows that you don't have time for anyone else. This allows him to get comfortable and monopolize your time. When he gets comfortable he might promise to call and then never do it. Or he might always call at the last minute with an impromptu plan. While this behavior can be exciting, understand that in his mind you are always available because you have nothing else to do. When you are too available, there is no pressure on him to be consistent in his attentions toward you. He can take whatever time he wants. He has no competition.

There is nothing to make him feel that he has to stay on his p's and q's and consider your time. Being too available isn't just for dates; it goes for phone calls as well. If you have all the time in the world to stay on the phone, he will have no urgency to see you. And if he has no urgency to see you, he has no urgency to have you. Got it?

TOO MUCH, TOO SOON

Another dynamic that takes the pressure off of him is getting involved in sex too soon. Let's be honest, if a man really is attracted to someone and really desires her for a mate, she also stimulates him sexually. This is a big factor in the pressure he is experiencing. Getting involved in sex too early relieves him of that pressure. Remember the testosterone jolt we mentioned earlier. A relationship with you has to cost him other relationships or characteristics that can otherwise hinder your relationship down the road. Self-control is an important feature for a man and should be on your nonnegotiable list. Remember the reason commitment is avoided or delayed is because it eliminates options, and no one eliminates options unless they have to. The reason he *has not* committed is because he *is not* committed.

PUTTING LOVE ON HOLD

We've all found a garment at a department store and asked the attendant to hold it. Why didn't you just buy it? Because you thought there might be something better in another store. You wanted to comparison shop. You felt comfortable taking your time because other choices were still available. If you didn't find anything better, you came back to buy the item. But if you found something more to your liking elsewhere, you would purchase it, leaving the first item temporarily unavailable to someone else. This is why stores give you a limited time period for holding your item. Seldom does the customer have the consideration to call the store and tell the salesclerk they no longer want the item, so holding something indefinitely would ultimately cost the store. Meanwhile, you've moved on with your new and better find.

Get the picture? Never put yourself on hold while someone shops around for someone more to his liking. He needs to know he can lose you. Never give away your power. Remember if he wants some*thing,* any woman will do, but if he has decided that you are the some*one* he wants, only you will do. Again, your power is in your uniqueness. The fact that there is only one of you, and if his hunger is for you, then only you will do. Never underestimate the power of attraction when a man wants you. This period of time is particularly effective to challenge a man to change. Remember: Everyone needs to change. If you don't change, you don't grow, and if you don't grow, you crystallize. A willingness to change is an essential element in a prospective mate.

Though a willingness to change is essential, you must also remember that God is not going to allow you to manage the change in your husband's life. Your position is merely to *inspire* it, not require it. You do this by setting a standard. Make it clear to him in a quiet way what is unacceptable to you. First Peter 3:1-5 speaks of the woman winning the man over without any words. *How will he change if I don't say anything?* you might wonder. He will be won over by observing your behavior. You can set a silent standard while maintaining a gentle and quiet spirit. No one changes until they are convinced they need to change. By observing your interaction with him, as well as with others, he should be saying to himself (without any prompting from you), "Man, I've got to get my act together if I want to be with this woman. She deserves more than what I'm putting out right now."

If the motivation to change is not present in the man you are considering, you will have a decision to make. You will have to look at him in his present state and ask yourself, "Could I be happy with him the way he is, even if he doesn't change?" Be honest with yourself. The things that are minute irritants now will be magnified in a marriage relationship. Can you deal forever with the things about him that bother you?

THEY THAT WAIT

Now be realistic, change takes time. Even God understands this. He is patient with us because he is not willing for us to perish. This, however, does not mean that he takes any old behavior from us lying down. Not at all. At times he even withdraws in order for us to experience the discomfort of not feeling his presence. It is in these moments that we decide to make the changes we know will please him, in order to restore closeness with him. Take a clue from the One who created patience. He does not rush change in our lives even though he does require it.

As the man in your life begins to indicate that he is attempting to adjust himself for your good, take the time to see whether his adjustments become permanent change. Don't get happy and begin to celebrate before the change has become a habit or second nature to him. Time reveals all things. Time separates facade from reality.

Have you ever been given an antibiotic when you had an infection? The doctor instructed you to complete the entire course of the prescription, whether you were feeling better or not, because a bacteria can hide latent in your system. If you don't kill it completely, it will resurface. If you are needy and willing to accept the first sign of change in a man, you will never see the work in him completed. Stand back and let him finish his course.

I (Michelle) have a friend who met a very attractive man who pursued her with fervor. She liked him, but he was not saved. She blatantly told him that she was attracted to him but that she couldn't have anything to do with him because her relationship with God was more important to her. Though his personality was great and his character admirable, his spiritual posture disqualified him from anything more than a friendship. Her rationale for not compromising was simply this: God had always been there and never let her down, while men had come and gone in her life. Why should she disappoint the One who had been faithful for someone she couldn't be sure of? This man chafed under her words, considered her self-right-eous, but would not give up.

He attended church with her and acted mildly interested in God, but then he would completely flip and ridicule her on some stand like celibacy. He would celebrate her gifts and encourage her in her ministry, then questioned her faith and the validity of the Bible. But he would not leave her alone.

She moved away to attend seminary, and he followed her. He made repairs on her home; he even drove her all the way from the East Coast back to Chicago when she got ill. The clash of the wills continued, but she refused to lower her standard. Finally, he accepted Jesus Christ as his Savior and submitted to counseling with the pastors at her school. Still, she waited. Proof for her that he had really changed inwardly came when he simply said, "I never realized the amount of profanity that occurred in my workplace before now! You know the world really makes it hard to be a gentleman. I can't stand how vulgar society has become." Nothing had changed at his workplace. It was *he* who had changed.

They will be married by the time this book comes out. She stood on her square for Jesus and did not budge, and the Lord declared checkmate on her behalf. She has a saved man who pursued her and who worked to gain her hand.

How many women are married to men who don't go to church? Just because a man attends a few Sundays while they are courting shouldn't convince a women that he will attend consistently once they are married. After a man gets what he wants, he will likely resort back to football games on Sundays instead. The deciding factor that indicates change is alive and well in the heart of your man is when he becomes the initiator of things you once had to suggest. Change is not change until it's change.

Things That Make You Go Hmmm...

- What compromises have you made with men in your life?

- Have those compromises gotten you what you wanted?

- What standards have you set for the man in your life to observe?

- Has your presence in his life made him want to be a better man for you?

- Are you willing to wait for a change? Do you trust God? Are you able to release this man into God's hands and allow God to finish the work?

- What do you think will happen if you stand your ground?

Chapter Eleven

The Maturity Factor

Rule #11: Separate the Men from the Boys

To be in love with someone who cannot love is a setup for heartbreak. Be confident he has the maturity to love from his heart as a decision, not just because he feels good. When someone says they are in love, it's a matter of attraction and discovery, but being *able* to love is an issue of maturity. God ties love to maturity in 1 Corinthians 13. Check the maturity level of your marriage prospect.

Realize that maturity does not come with age but with acceptance of responsibility. Antoine de Saint-Exupery, the French author who penned *The Little Prince,* observed, "To be a man is, precisely, to be responsible." He went on to explain that there is no growth except in the fulfillment of obligations. Responsibility is the ability to respond to problems. Change is normal to life, and change normally happens in crisis. Change happens this way because crisis highlights reality and shows where changes must occur. If change is normal to life, crisis is also a normal occurrence. Your husband should be the chief problem-solver in your life, so how he responds in crisis is important. The difference between responsible and irresponsible people is how they see things. Responsible people see what they can do or could have done to make a situation better. They look for solutions. Irresponsible people automatically see what *others* can do or could have done to make the situation better. While responsible people look for solutions, irresponsible people look for a place to lay blame. Solving the problem is less important to them than establishing that they are not at fault.

A story goes that once upon a time there was a man by the name of Samson. Samson sounds as if he would have been any woman's dream: tall, strong, and fine. He was a judge in Israel. However, Samson was a man given to following his lust. He was hardheaded, did not take advice, and did not respect his parents. He was not the most discerning man. He was hot-tempered and impulsive. Samson was a spoiled brat. If we were to sum up everything about Samson in one word we would simply say, *immature.*

The events that led to his undoing are told in Judges 14–15. Samson saw a woman he decided he had to have. Against the advice of his parents—who were concerned about him marrying someone who wasn't a believer in God and worse yet a Philistine (an enemy of Israel)—he married her. At their wedding feast he came up with a riddle for the wedding guests that would cost them dearly if they didn't come up with the answer. So the wedding guests threatened his new bride to give them the answer. His bride then proceeded to nag him until she got the answer out of him. Promptly she told the guests. At the appointed time, they served up the right answer. In his rage that his own wife had betrayed him, Samson went on a killing spree, left his wife, and returned to his parent's house.

After a while Samson got lonely and went back to claim his bride, only to find out that her father, who thought that Samson no longer wanted her, had given the young lady to the best man to marry. Did Samson stop to consider his role in this misunderstanding? No, his very revealing words were, "This time I shall be blameless regarding the Philistines if I harm them!"(15:3, NKJV). Off he went on another murderous mission to destroy the fields of the Philistines. When the Philistines asked who was responsible for all of this costly damage, they were told, "Samson, the son-in-law of the Timnite, because he [the father-in-law] has taken his wife and given her to his companion" (15:6, NKJV). So the Philistines went and got the woman and her father and burned them to death. Samson's immaturity cost him the life of his wife and her family. Later, when he met up with Delilah, his refusal to learn and mature would cost him his own life.

The moral of this story? Immaturity in your man will affect your life and could ultimately cost you everything. Sometimes immaturity will have an adverse affect on your family and then spread beyond your house to affect others you love.

Responsible people feel the pressure to fix things. Irresponsible people seek to relieve that pressure through excuses and fault finding. That's why irresponsible people never change: it's never their fault; they are not the ones who need to change. If you could change their parents, their teachers, their race, give them more money, and so on, everything would be all right. Simply said, nothing is ever their fault.

If you marry an irresponsible person, you will instantly be the major reason for his unhappiness. An irresponsible man does not have the ability to respond in a crisis. If he caves in to the pressure of advances by another woman, you will be blamed because you gained weight, weren't sensitive enough, or did any one thing he can use as an excuse to escape his own guilt. He will leave you feeling not pretty enough, not woman enough, and doubting your value—when all the time he was just weak and immature.

You've heard that opposites attract. Irresponsible people look for responsible people to marry. In most cases, when a man disappoints a woman, she sees him as evil and plotting to hurt her. More often than not, however, he just doesn't have the inner strength to handle the pressure of temptation. When a man's physical body matures, he develops strength that we call muscles. As the inner man matures, he should develop inner muscles as well, which we call character or maturity or responsibility. The outer man can make a baby, but the inner man chooses whether to be a father in accordance with his level of maturity.

OF MEN AND CHILDREN

Some women fail to distinguish between sincerity and character. They detect that a man is sincere and begin to trust him. But he may not have the character to keep his word. The pressure produced by a need for money will push a person to take out a loan believing they will diligently pay back the loan. In fact, they will sign their name to a contract saying so. The question becomes, once they have the money in hand and the pressure is relieved, will repayment of the loan still be a priority, or will the pressure to continue spending overshadow their commitment to the bank?

Pressure can motivate any of us to make a promise in order to obtain something. But do we have the character to keep our promise after the pressure is off? This was the thinking behind layaway plans before the use of credit cards became so prevalent. The store knew your passion to possess that thing would make you keep those payments coming until you were able to claim the item. Likewise, the pressure a man initially feels to possess you can cause him to make promises he is unable to keep. Yes, there is a difference between a broken promise and a lie. But the result is the same. A man does not have to be a liar to break your heart. There is a difference between sincere intention and mature follow through.

This kind of behavior is precisely why banks check your credit (your track record). They know that what people have done in the past, they tend to do in the future. People do change, of course, but banks don't invest in potential, they invest in patterns. A bank won't give money to a person who has proven unreliable. Why would you give your life to a man whose pattern indicates the same? When a husband acts like a child, his behavior forces his wife to act like his mother. This interaction adversely affects their intimacy—no healthy man is sexually attracted to his mother.

Every man needs to read 1 Corinthians 13:11. It says, "When I was a child, I talked like a child, I thought like a child, I reasoned like a child. When I became a man, I put childish ways behind me." One version of this verse says, "But on becoming a man I was through with childish ways" (MLB). God encourages us to come to him as a child, which indicates unconditional trust, but he then encourages us to be mature in our relationships with one another.

I (Joel) learned the characteristics of a child from one of my spiritual mentors, Ed Cole. Here's the list: center of his own universe, insensitive to others, having temper tantrums, irresponsible, noncommunicative, demands his own way, only subject to concrete authority. Let's take a deeper look at each of these traits.

Center of his own universe. A man is called to love his wife. This means putting her first. God does not give man the headship to boss everybody around. Headship calls for him to become the chief servant. Jesus said that the least would be greatest, therefore, he should be servant, leader, and head. The decisions he makes should always put his family first. With a childish man, what *he* wants comes first. A childish man is the center of *his* universe and believes that he is the center of *the* universe. Everything that happens must ultimately serve him. If something doesn't make him happy, he makes sure that nobody is happy. He feels entitled to how he feels and that you should understand. If you don't, you are the villain.

Insensitive to others. To lead a household, a man needs to be sensitive to others, including God, his family, and the people in his work environment. An insensitive man is not going to pray or read his

Bible unless he happens to feel like it. He will upset the atmosphere in his home just because he is unhappy. Because he is insensitive in the workplace, he may lose jobs, suffer in his career, and never understand why. Though he may be insensitive to your needs, he will be touchy and easily offended when it comes to his own.

Temper tantrums. One quality of a childish man is that when he can't make people do what he wants, he becomes a "terrorist." We

BOTH SIDES OF THE STORY

The adulterous man is irresponsible and immature. He blames his bad marriage on his spouse and uses this excuse to seduce other vulnerable women. Every single woman explains the infidelity of the man she's stealing in the same way: "He's unhappy. His wife doesn't treat him properly. They aren't getting along." It is not *your* responsibility to make that man feel good. It is *his* responsibility to do whatever is necessary to reconcile with his wife.

Have you ever considered what the married man did to make his wife become unresponsive? Or have you ever considered what the situation might be at his house and how he contributed to it? In most cases, if you heard both sides of the story, you would conclude that these two people deserved each other and that whatever the problem was, God allowed it to encourage change or growth in both of them. They simply refused to take responsibility for the changes that their relationship demanded.

call it "going off." One form of his terror can be spousal abuse. We're not saying that people who hit their wives don't have other problems, but the chief problem is immaturity. I (Joel) remember talking to a man once who had hit his wife. When I asked him why, he replied, "She knows how to push my buttons." I asked him where his buttons were, so that I could push them. After getting in his face and trying to push his buttons, I couldn't get him to hit me. He didn't have any buttons at all. He was just a little boy who beat up on girls. Everyone thought this man was out of control, needing counseling or even deliverance, but his problem was not mental or demonic. He was not out of control. Hitting his wife was simply a strategy he used to get what he wanted.

Irresponsible. We've discussed this topic, but we'll add one thing. Childish men call responsibility pressure. When you attempt to hold them accountable to their word or their duty, they complain about being pressured.

Noncommunicative. This man expects the woman in his life to go the second and third mile to solve his problems, but when she has a problem, it is her problem. He is childish and unreasonable and moody. When he is unhappy, rather than tell you what's wrong, he sulks, broods, and makes everyone miserable until somebody finally asks him what is wrong. Then he gets to tell you, at your request, about all the people who are not treating him properly. He has a mental list of all the things that are needed to make him happy, but you have to interview, study him, and go fishing in his mind for information he could just tell you. Some take noncommunication to the extreme. They continue to say, "Nothing," when asked what's wrong. You have to have ESP for these people. If you don't solve the problem that they haven't vocalized, they make you part of the problem too.

Demands his own way. Not only will a childish man put himself first, but he will also demand that everyone else put him first. So you will always watch the television show he wants to see, eat at his favorite restaurant, go to his favorite spot for vacation (even if there is nothing for you and the children to do there), and leave when he is ready, even if no one else is. You will forever be on his personal agenda.

Only subject to concrete authority. A childish man cannot be reasoned with. He will not respond to authority unless motivated by the consequences rather than the principle. This is the man who refuses to go to counseling until his wife threatens to leave, who only straightens up at work when he faces losing his job. In extreme cases, this man might not forsake unhealthy habits until he is faced with a danger to himself or the possibility of incarceration. Doing right because it is right is not in his repertoire. His behavior may change when he is in the doghouse because he wants to get out, not because he wants to make you happy.

And now let's contrast God's idea of what a mature man looks like:

God-centered vs. self-centered. God is at the center of his life, his worldview, and his decisions. This man bases his life on God's Word and the rules that God gives for relationships. He responds to difficulty according to God's direction and not by what he feels. He is not arrogant or selfish. He is able to serve for the betterment of everyone, even though it may cost him.

Sensitive to others. This man is not rude. He considers others above himself. He is patient and kind. He is motivated by your need and slow to point out your faults. He attempts to make you feel secure and is sensitive to your weaknesses.

Self-controlled. A mature man does not have temper tantrums. He does not feel the need to demonstrate his displeasure by upsetting the atmosphere with shifting moods and unpleasant behavior. He walks in discipline in his personal life and does nothing that would encourage you to compromise your godly standards. He understands the difference between being spontaneous and being compulsive.

Responsible. A mature man does not run from pressure. He is a problem-solver. When there is a need, he steps up to the plate and follows through with decisive action. He is also able to admit when he is wrong and rejoice when you are right. He is able to receive correction as well as give it. He is aware of his God-ordained responsibility toward a woman and is moved to protect and provide for her. He is reliable and can be trusted.

Open and communicative. A mature man tells you at all times what is on his mind and where he is. If he is going through a difficult period, you don't have to guess what is going on. He initiates discussion about his difficulties in a non-accusing way and is open to your thoughts in working out a solution.

Submitted to authority. A mature man respects authority and is motivated by principle. He does the right thing because it is the right thing to do. He does not abuse his own authority, because he understands the principle of leading by serving. Just as Christ loved the church and gave himself for it even though he was lord over it, this man will give himself for you and be an authority you can yield to because his leadership is based on love.

When considering the man in your life, check the list. If the numbers don't add up, subtract yourself from the relationship. The bottom line is that you cannot change him—don't even try it. When dating, leave your mothering instincts at home. If you don't, the immature man will take advantage of your nurturing, and the mature man will respond negatively to it. Stay focused on what you are looking for: a husband, a priest, a lover, a cover. A man who can handle the job description. So make it clear by the way that you carry yourself that little boys need not apply.

Things That Make You Go Hmmm...

- Are you dating a man or a boy?

- How does pressure make him respond?

- Does he cast blame or become introspective when problems crop up?

- In moments of difficulty, does he partner with you to work through the problem, or does he become defensive and accusing?

- Is he open to dealing with issues truthfully?

Chapter Twelve

The Other Side of Attraction: His

Rule #12: Know How to Work It

Long before there was the Miss America Pageant, another great pageant was held in search of a queen for a king. The book of Esther tells us the story of a search sent out from India to Ethiopia for beautiful young virgins that would be brought before the king. But before these women ever entered the king's presence to audition for his heart and the coveted crown, they were submitted to twelve months of beauty treatments—a special diet, exceptional baths and massages with essential oils and herbs, hours spent with hairdressers and tailors and teachers of the arts. After this time of preparation, each woman would select whatever clothing and jewelry she wanted to enhance her beauty before seeing the king. Esther was one of these women. If the king liked her and enjoyed her company, she would be chosen. If he did not, she would be taken to the second harem and kept with the rest of his concubines. He wouldn't throw her away, but he would keep her available while still in pursuit of what he really wanted. Does this sound familiar to you?

Esther watched the parade of women going in and out of the king's chambers until finally her own turn came. Instead of following the pattern of the other women, Esther turned to Hegai, the eunuch in charge of the harem, and asked his advice as to what she should wear. She had the foresight to find out what the king was looking for before she made her selection of attire. If you want to catch a man's attention, you've got to be what he is looking for. "But what is he looking for?" you ask. Beauty inside and out.

In this story, a search was made for virgins, but don't condemn yourself if you are no longer a virgin. It is the spirit of a woman that a man senses. He wants a woman who every man wants but every man has not had. Contrary to popular belief, every man is not looking for a freak (as we described in chapter 5). He would be pleased to find that you are comfortable with your sexuality and uninhibited in the marriage bed, but he does not want that on display to the rest of the world. Neither does he want it to be popular knowledge.

In Song of Songs (in the Bible), one of the juiciest books of poetry you'd ever want to read, the Lover proudly says of his Beloved, "You are a garden locked up, my sister, my bride; you are a spring enclosed, a sealed fountain" (4:12). This woman had kept her delights off-limits to others, and he was the only one permitted to enter. In this same book, the woman's brothers ask her if she has been a wall or a door. If she has been a wall and kept herself pure, they will crown her with honor. If she has been a door, allowing men to enter her, they would enclose her in cedar, or condemn her to death. She confidently replies, "I am a wall, and my breasts are like towers. Thus I have become in his eyes like one bringing contentment" (8:10). She is saying that she has kept herself pure, that she stands and walks proudly because she has no shame. Because of this, her man is content. He knows he can trust her. A man looks for a woman he can trust.

After Solomon asked, "Who can find a virtuous wife?" in Proverbs 31:10 (NKJV), the rest of the chapter explains that the reason she was such a valuable find was because the heart of her husband could safely trust in her. A man does not want a woman he has to question or worry about. If a woman gives her body to a man too soon, he will always wonder how many others she has given herself to. However, if she loves him and won't compromise herself sexually with him before marriage, his ego tells him that if he couldn't get it, no one can!

This will be the last time we address sex, so we will close this subject with a strong reminder that your body does not belong to you. In God's eyes, you are already engaged to his Son, who paid a bride-price for you. Until Christ releases you into the arms of the one he has chosen to be the physical manifestation of his love for you, he considers any sexual relationship you have to be adultery. You would not (or should not) sleep around before your wedding, so therefore conduct yourself as a woman who presently belongs to someone— you belong to Christ.

Esther was chosen not just because she was beautiful. All the women were beautiful. Esther was chosen because she set herself apart from the others. First, she found out what the king liked and adjusted herself accordingly. After she had passed the outer test, the king took the time to examine her more closely. He liked what he saw, what he heard, and how he felt in her presence. *All* of these factors influence the heart of the man who chooses to commit to you, so let's examine them in detail.

ON THE OUTSIDE LOOKING IN

The unfortunate thing is that at first glance, a man cannot see your heart. Therefore, if you don't turn his head to begin with, you may never get to show it to him. Men are visually stimulated, so you cannot ignore your physical appearance. What a man considers attractive is subjective, depending on culture, values, the media, and so on. The guidelines we are going to discuss are not absolute truths, but they do speak to strong tendencies in women that cause their own hurt.

What we are about to say may be painful, but we would not be serving you if we didn't address this issue. As a man, I (Joel) know several women who are great people. They are good Christians, loyal, loving, great parents, productive, successful, yet they are not married. Some are frustrated because they feel they are missing out on marriage. Some even have a subtle resentment toward God for not bringing them a mate. A pastor friend and I were talking one day about this subject, and I found that several women in his congregation whom I had known for some time were now engaged. I jokingly said that maybe his church had found the secret to praying for husbands. He replied that the secret was much less spiritual. They had joined a local spa, lost weight, gotten fit, felt better, looked better, became confident, and thus, more attractive, and were now engaged.

Never underestimate the importance of weight and other appearance issues when it comes to men. You can be a great person with a great personality, but when someone describes you as a prospective love interest to someone else and only mentions your personality, that person will know there are problems elsewhere. Yes, some men prefer heavier women. But there is a difference between preference and conviction.

I (Joel) may prefer a certain kind of woman, but I am convicted that I should marry someone with strong Christian beliefs, good character, and values similar to mine. Under pressure, preferences change, but convictions should grow stronger. If a man has the proper values, his desire to marry you may override his preference for certain physical attributes. I have met several attractive, heavy women who feel good about themselves, and that confidence is sexy. They are able to get away with wearing things the average heavy person would shy away from, and they are able to pull it off with style. That extra appeal is in the way they carry themselves and in their attention to grooming.

We are not saying that skinny is godly and that heavy is ungodly. *Healthy* is godly. You should be the best you that you can be. Develop habits that make you the healthiest person you can be. Rather than going on diets to try to look a certain way, cultivate a good diet and exercise regimen that will become a lifestyle. When you have a healthy lifestyle, well-documented health risks, like those associated with being overweight or sedentary, will often decline or disappear. When you are healthy, you will feel good. The better you feel, the better you will look. The better you look, the greater your self-esteem.

I (Joel) remember one person I was dating who kept commenting on how surprised she was that she was attracted to me since she was usually attracted to buff guys. She was trying to pay me a compliment, but I didn't feel great when she said it. Actually, it hurt, and she eventually quit saying it. I have since lost thirty pounds and am on my way to "buff-hood," but I'm doing it more for health reasons than for marriage.

SILENT SIGNALS

Let's establish the difference between style and excellence. Style is a personal thing, a cultural issue. Your personal style expresses who you are as a person. It reflects what's going on inside of you. You can tell a lot about people by the way they dress. Disorder on the outside usually indicates disorder on the inside. Artsy people wear unique things. Conservative dressers are usually conservative people. We all like to experiment with clothing but very seldom does anyone stray over the bounds of their comfort level. Sometimes in an effort to be seductive, women cross that line and then feel insulted when they get the wrong feedback from a man. "How dare he think I was loose!" they exclaim. But that is what their clothing insinuated. A woman

By the way, appearance can hint at something else—discipline, and discipline is a character issue. A lack of discipline, as it relates to our body being the temple of God, could be a hint at a character problem that needs to be addressed. But if you are healthy, the size you should be, and a certain man is not attracted to you, then he is not for you. This doesn't mean you want to risk not being the best you can be, because you might miss out on an opportunity for someone to discover your real beauty.

Now this is going to get a little touchy for some of you, but men like hair they can touch, hair they can mess up. They want to know

needs to pay attention to dress and determine whether she is sending mixed signals to a man.

Ever notice that the same clothes that get a man to turn his head to look at another woman are the very same he will not allow *his* woman to wear? Though he may have found what he saw interesting to look at, he understands that conclusions are drawn based on what you wear, and he doesn't want those conclusions drawn about *his* woman.

What type of impression do you want to make on a man? Dress accordingly. Though style may be a matter of personal taste and choice, it goes beyond you. People take their cue from the way you dress. Your style will attract people who have similar tastes as you. So make your wardrobe work to your benefit.

there will be no zones that are off-limits to them when you become theirs. Having to be cognizant of a woman's hair while making love robs the moment of the spontaneity that could make it special. It takes the fun out of the moment. It's like a football player with a clean uniform. A dirty uniform for a football player is proof that he got some action. Some hairdos are either indestructible or so delicate that to touch them would cause a crisis. This might seem as if it's too personal an issue to discuss here, but it's important. And indeed it is very subjective, but the last poll taken indicates that for most men, a woman with a hairdo that feels more like a helmet than actual hair would be a deal-breaker. We are not suggesting that you take on any particular style but that you be the best person you can be with whatever style you choose. Be soft. Be approachable. Be touchable.

Everything that you decide to wear or apply should enhance and not detract. You should be well groomed so that your natural beauty shines through. A bright healthy smile (is it time for braces?) can really work for you. But balance is the key. There is such pressure on women to look glamorous that some have crossed the line and wear clothing that is too revealing. This doesn't have to be you. Dress and carry yourself to attract the kind of man you want. You can turn a man's head without turning his heart, *but* if you don't turn his head, you may not get to his heart. Be balanced.

Need some helpful hints? Don't ask your women friends. You would be surprised to find that what seems attractive to a woman is not what is attractive to a man. Men are not impressed with tons of makeup; they just imagine a mess being left on them. Skimpy clothing, contrary to popular belief, is not the answer. But things that leave a man guessing and wanting to see more are always appealing— soft colors that bring out the best in you and soften your persona, nice lines that suggest more than they show. When in doubt, ask the advice of brothers and other male friends. They will give you the real deal on how you look. They will tell you what they think brings out the best of your feminine self. Take your cues from that information and run with it. Don't dash off and run up the credit cards with new clothes and makeup; simply develop the habit of being your best. Be healthy, be clean, look good, smell good—and be attractive.

TAKING PERSONAL INVENTORY

We have taught you in previous chapters to be intentional and to have a vision—to make out the list of attributes that you want in a relationship. Your prospective husband also has a list, whether written or unwritten. What's on his list? Take a personal inventory. Do you feel you fit the list of positive attributes that someone else may have? Take stock of the negatives in your life—being out of shape, bad habits like smoking or being messy, bad hygiene, poor money habits like overspending and debt, undisciplined children. These are not on the lists of the man you want to marry.

The best way to attract what you are looking for is to *be* what you are looking for yourself. You attract what you are. It is highly unlikely, if you are not physically together, that you will attract someone who is the body beautiful. So work on yourself, take advantage of your singleness to improve yourself, not simply for the sake of a man, but for you. You want to feel good, look good, and have your life in order for yourself. In looking to join your life with another, consider what you are offering. Some women don't want to be married; they want to be rescued. They have unruly children, money problems, and want a knight in shining armor to come and rescue them from what they don't want to deal with themselves. No man is looking for a bad situation. Everybody is looking for someone to add to life and make it more enjoyable.

Some people are rescuers and drawn to people with chronic problems, but the relationships that develop this way are unhealthy and rarely lead to happiness. Be the best that you can be—inside and out—and let the rest fall into place.

THE WAY TO A MAN'S HEART

A man commits based on how he feels in your presence. If you believe that God will supply you with a mate, it makes sense that you will come across this person while you are doing God's will. That setting allows a man to observe you more closely. I (Joel) have ministered at various churches where someone has caught my eye. When I asked about one gorgeous lady, the pastor's response was, "She is a good person but her walk has not been consistent." The recommendation was less than glowing, so I did not proceed any further. This woman never knew I was interested. Many women never realize that their demeanor or the wrong kind of friends or habits may have cost them what could have possibly been a great relationship. Ruth was simply serving her mother-in-law, with no other motive but to serve, when Boaz noticed her. This act of devotion positioned her for her destiny. You never know when your Boaz may be watching.

Be in position. Be in place. Be found doing the will of God with a consistent life and commendable character, as opposed to wanting to get your life together after meeting a good Christian man. If you are walking in the purpose God has designed for your life, you will have a God appointment. You will happen on the place that puts you in plain view of your mate. So check your motivation for being

FIVE ESSENTIALS IN THE HEART OF A MAN

There are five qualities that should be present in the heart of a man you are considering for a mate:

1. He should be moved to provide for you.

2. He should be moved to protect you.

3. He should see himself as the solution to your needs or problems.

4. He should guard your reputation.

5. He should have to go through something to get you, not because you are a victim, but because you are a good woman.

All of these elements came together in the heart of Boaz in the story of the young widow, Ruth.

where you are. Is your intention to be productive for the sake of God's kingdom? If your answer is yes, you will be in the right place at the right time. Or are you going to that church just because a bunch of good-looking single men go there?

The Bible tells us that Ruth *happened* upon the ground that belonged to Boaz. She thought she was just gleaning the fields for food. Her focus was on doing what she needed to do for the sake of survival, but all the time God was preparing a mate for her. Based on her willingness to be productive, Boaz was moved to provide for her. It is important to note that she did not tell Boaz she needed anything. She was busy making a way for herself. Yet this stirred his heart to help her. Your productivity is important to the man who is considering you as a partner. No man wants a woman who does not exhibit the capacity to function in times of stress or lack. It makes him feel that if he hit a crisis in his own life, you would fall apart. He doesn't want to be your oxygen, but he *does* want to sweeten the fragrance of the air around you. He does not want to *rescue* you, but he does want to *join* you. He doesn't want to *carry* you, but he does want to *cover* you. There is a difference. A healthy man wants to join his strength to your strength—not to your weakness. He does not seek to control you or be controlled by you. He is in search of a complimentary partnership. We said that your life should be better because of him, but the opposite is also true: His life should be better because of you.

I (Joel) know of several men who were deeply in love with

women who needed them desperately: emotionally and financially. They found themselves being the knight in shining armor to rescue them from loneliness, poverty, fatherless children, and uncertain futures, only to find a few months into the relationship that their involvement with these women was sucking the life out of them. They in turn needed to be rescued from these women. Any account—whether a bank account or an emotional account—that experiences more withdrawals than deposits will become bankrupt. Make sure you're able to make a healthy deposit into the relationship.

TIMING IS EVERYTHING

Putting yourself in the right *place* is important, but being there is ineffective if you're not there at the right *time*. For example, in Ruth's story, Naomi senses God's hand at work and instructs Ruth on how to respond to this favor. She tells Ruth to wash up, put on her best clothes, go to where Boaz is, and wait until he has finished eating and drinking. Naomi's instructions seem rather curious at first, but a little investigation reveals that she gave Ruth those instructions because she knew that Ruth shouldn't approach Boaz until he was "in good spirits" and ready to hear Ruth's proposal (see Ruth 3).

A person's state of mind is significant when you are trying to sell them on a new idea. You must do it in the right atmosphere. There are certain times to talk about certain subjects, and then there are other times when you should hold your peace. Timing is everything.

Never try to persuade someone to do something when they are in a negative or unsettled state of mind.

On a side note, some may say that Ruth seduced Boaz. That is definitely not the case. Seduction is similar to witchcraft. It is the use of soulful skill or craft to bring someone under your power and to push them to do something that they do not want to do or know they should not do. Seduction is based on lust and is meant to manipulate and use. Seduction is ungodly and should never be a tool for the believer. And lust is a desire to benefit oneself at another's expense. Proverbs 7:21 says that the adulterous woman seduced the naive man with her lips. Seduction is a force that is evil. What Ruth did was not evil. And Ruth was not a lustful person. Ruth was a serving person, which was how she was noticed.

TO PURSUE OR NOT TO PURSUE

Ruth didn't pursue either. In an earlier chapter we stated that it is improper for a woman to pursue a man because it makes her vulnerable. It puts her at risk of not being valued or at risk of being used, and it allows for experimentation on the man's part. On the other hand, once the man has noticed a woman and she has his attention, she definitely wants to let him know that she's interested. Men's egos tend to be fragile. Some men will pursue relentlessly until they capture the woman. Other men are concerned about being attractive to the woman of their dreams and will pursue more subtly. Men don't want to be tolerated; they want to be celebrated. So, if a man senses early on that a woman is not attracted to him or has no desire for him, he will move on.

Be encouraging but not desperate. God led Ruth to be put in a position for Boaz to notice her, then Ruth responded with her encouragement. Show interest but do not initiate it. Be interest*ed* and interest*ing.* If a man has passed all of your tests and has made it known that he is attracted to you and wants to pursue things further, respond in ways that will encourage him. A desire to please your mate is a quality you will need in marriage. This should be present at the onset, as with Ruth. Her actions were the catalyst to what would eventually become a history-making marriage. Pleasing a man is more art than science, but pleasing a man should not become a preoccupation.

Our discussion here may give you the impression that you should be distant or aloof. We are not saying you should appear stuck-up or difficult. If you are playing hard to get, you will be hard to get. So don't do that. We are trying to help you find the love of your life and get married. So, simply put, be choosy. Be intentional about what you want and what qualifies a man to be with you. Use the tools we have given you to eliminate people who are not good for you, to avoid wasting your time, and to sidestep heartache.

To put it all together: Make sure that you look your best, that you *are* your best, and that you are encouraging. Your strength is in your uniqueness. The way God made you is the way he wants you.

He may want to temper some things but not douse them completely. He is perfectly tailoring you, not only for your destiny, but for the person he has ordained for you to be with. Make sure that you cultivate what counts—a strong "inner self, the unfading beauty of a gentle and quiet spirit, which is of great worth in God's sight" (1 Peter 3:4). These are irresistible traits that will draw the man for you.

Never remake yourself for anyone other than God or try to be someone other than who you are. Being someone other than who you are naturally will tax your energy. Eventually you will run out of gas for the relationship and feel resentment toward the person for whom you have changed. When a man demands that you change in order to be with him, he is merely camouflaging rejection. Rather than rejecting you and moving on, he rejects you and tries to make you into the person he is looking for. Suggest he go in search of that other person. The loss of a relationship is nothing compared to the loss of yourself.

Remember, "Charm is deceptive, and beauty is fleeting; but a woman who fears the LORD is to be praised" (Proverbs 31:30). The hearts of men and kings is in the Lord's hands, and he is able to turn their hearts whichever way he wishes. When a man or woman's ways please the Lord, he promises to make even their enemies live at peace with them. If he is able to cause your enemies to look upon you favorably, how much more will he bless you by turning the heart of a good man in your direction? That's your cue. Make sure that when the right man looks your way, he is able to agree with God and say, "It is good."

Things That Make You Go Hmmm...

- How do you feel about yourself when you look in the mirror? Are the things that displease you things that you can do something about?

- Are you in, or on your way to, optimum health?

- What type of men are you attracting? Are they attracted to the inner or the outer you?

- Are there unnecessary liabilities attached to you that could be a turnoff?

- Have you cultivated the domestic skills to make a house a home? If not, why?

- Do you feel you are in the will of God for your life? Why or why not? What would your Boaz say about you if he were watching you from afar?

Chapter Thirteen

The Power of a Woman

Rule #13: Use Your Power Wisely

Now that you've gotten the man's attention, what do you do? Find your power, and use it. What makes a man an overcomer? Primarily his connection to God. But his connection to the right woman, too, can be pivotal. That's where our power lies. So it makes sense that Satan would attack the relationship between men and women in an effort to keep us apart and unfruitful.

In the last twenty years, society has promoted in women what it may label strength but what is really hardness. So much pressure on a woman has forced her to forsake her *power* in relationships. When you abandon your power, you become truly hard, weak, immoral, seductive, insensitive, and/or overly demanding. These hardness characteristics violate your femininity, your nature, and your person. Contrary to society's view, *hard* does not translate into strong, and *soft* does not translate into weak. In fact, hard objects are frequently brittle objects that can crumble under pressure, while soft objects are able to bend and rebound under the same pressure.

Society has also perverted the meaning of *power,* which we use in this context to mean God-given influence. How do women retrieve God's gift of power that has been lost? The answer is actually quite simple: They will regain their power in relationships by doing away with destructive thinking and by returning to the basics of God's design for them as women. Galatians 5:22-23, verses we refer to several times in this book, gives us a picture of how we are supposed to be: loving, joyful, peaceful, patient, kind, good, faithful, gentle, and full of self-control. Any characteristic that violates these fruits of the spirit is ungodly.

You have the power to turn a man's heart from boyhood to manhood; to turn his heart, hopefully, *toward* God through who you are. This power is not meant to be used to evangelize the man. This power was given to woman not to *lead* man but to *stabilize* him. God's observation that a man needed a woman in Genesis 2 suggests that men are better *with* women than they are *without* women. Statistics even state that men live longer when they are married. A woman completes a man and stabilizes his life. Marriage equips him to do what he was created to do first—be a true worshipper of God. If a man is sincerely attracted to you and you have his heart, then you should use this power productively towards God's purposes and not your own.

A real man is looking for a godly woman. He's not looking for hardness in a woman; he's searching for true strength.

BRING SOMETHING TO THE PARTY

We quoted Proverbs 18:22 earlier, which says, "He who finds a wife finds what is good and receives favor from the LORD." But why exactly is a wife a good thing?

A wife is a good thing because she was created to complete a man (this isn't to say she can't initiate anything). Other than the obvious physical differences, a woman can do or be anything a man can do or be. If a woman works the same job as a man, she should make the same pay. But biblically speaking, distinctions are made between the roles for men and women, primarily relating to the home and the church. And when it comes to male-female relationships, men and women are different by design. Women have not been designed weaker than men; they have been designed with different strengths. A woman expresses strength differently than a man does. She can accomplish the same objectives, but she does it in a different way.

Women are blessed with a broad range of abilities and talents. That is part of the mystery. Women have an amazing ability to take a vision, refine it, advance it, and complete it. God knows that. He created you that way and made these skills inherent to your very nature, enabling you to complement the man. Men tend to deal with the bottom line and with life in broad strokes. This sometimes blinds them to the finer details and intuitive aspects of decision making. This is why the Bible says it is not good for man to be alone. A good woman is a stabilizing and balancing force in the life of a man.

A wise woman once said that men fight with fists, and women fight with words. Overstating your case or the wrong use of your tongue can castrate a man and deliver severe blows to his person. This kind of behavior will only get you rejected. Remember Michal, David's wife (see 2 Samuel 6:16-23)? She cut him to shreds with her words right after he experienced one of his greatest victories: recovering the ark of God. He arrived home high on emotion, intending to bless everyone in his house, and she cut him down with a critical, scathing tongue. In that one moment, she fell from grace in his eyes. He told her that if she wanted to withhold praise from him, he would get it elsewhere. The story of their relationship ends with the sad comment that she remained unloved and childless for the rest of her days. All that negativity and criticism will get you nowhere with a real man.

Remember, you are just as powerful as he is, perhaps more so, but in a different way. Know that the subtle power you have as a woman is far more effective than your trying to force an issue. The man in your life is there for a reason. He is there because he wants to be. Be a help and a blessing to him.

The second greatest quality that caused Solomon to say a virtuous woman was worth more than rubies was the fact that she would help her husband and would not hinder him all of her days. So have wisdom for a man. Pray for him. Listen to God on his behalf. That is how a woman brings favor and blessings to a man. Be a source of consistency to his life and he will consistently want to be in yours. Proverbs advises men to stay away from a woman who is given to change, someone who is moody, difficult, and unstable.

The second chapter of Genesis says that the woman is made as a helper, or a helpmeet—someone who has what it takes to meet his needs and complete the man. Remember, this role of helper is in relationship to the man in the home. A woman can own her own business, run a school or a church, and function in any calling God has for her. Many women earn more money than the men in their lives, and it is up to each couple to decide exactly how they will relate to each other, taking stock of their various strengths and weaknesses and coming up with a strategy that best serves them. These issues are not vocational but relational.

Always play to his strength. Be a blessing and not a hindrance to him. This wisdom will help you discern what his values are, his priorities, and what he holds dear.

NOT EVERY PURSUING MAN IS FOR YOU

I (Michelle) have been in situations where men pursued me and I led them to Christ. None of these relationships resulted in marriage, as I am still single at this time. Please understand that every man who pursues you will not be for you. However, your call is the same as it would be for a sister to that man, to turn his heart toward God. Prepare him to be a good man for another woman. Who knows, someone might be doing the same thing for you. Remember that you reap what you sow. God will not overlook your seed, especially if they are sown directly into the kingdom.

Listen closely to him. The things he wants in life—are you willing and able to help him accomplish them? Do his goals excite you? Are you willing to help him achieve his vision, reach his destiny? What are positive attributes you see in him that he doesn't even know himself—strengths, talents, abilities? Do you see his potential? Do you see the hand of God in his life? Are you willing to complement him and see the will of God come to fruition in his life? Can you sense where God is taking him and use your influence to stabilize and help keep him on track? Not only do you love him, but do you love what he is *about*? If he is smart, he will sense it when you do. These are all important aspects of a godly relationship.

If you don't agree with his heart or his vision, you will have the power to get him off track. You should begin to study him and provide input in his life that will benefit him and advance his purpose and destiny. Remember, as we said in an earlier chapter, if he has your heart, he has you. That works both ways: If he is wise and sees you as an inspiration and a stabilizer, a helper in reaching his vision, those qualities will endear you to him. And if you have his heart, you have him.

THE GIFT OF ENCOURAGEMENT

We've touched on the spiritual and emotional ways to a man's heart. Now let's take a look at the natural ways. What draws the heart of a man to a woman? Or put in practical terms, why does a man run off with his secretary? The answer is simpler than you think. The secretary helps him achieve his dreams. A man is drawn to the woman who helps him complete his assignment in life, the one God created him for. So the strongest tool a woman can use is her ability to hear a man's dreams and translate them into real life accomplishment through her gift of encouragement. In other words, hear his heart, inspire him in the things of God, and help him achieve his life vision.

In order to encourage a man, you must first hear him. As we mentioned previously, "Out of the abundance of the heart the mouth speaks" (Matthew 12:34, NKJV). What is in his heart will definitely come out of his mouth. Once, when a man I (Michelle) was seeing asked me why I didn't ask him a lot of questions about himself, I replied, "If I interview you, you will only tell me what you think I want to hear. But if I listen long enough, I will learn more about you because you will talk about what is most important to you." What people talk about constantly is a major revealer of the heart.

Proverbs 20:5 says, "The purposes of a man's heart are deep waters, but a man [or woman] of understanding draws them out." Usually the answers to our life issues are already inside of us, placed there by the Holy Spirit. Counsel concerning the issues of someone's heart is not a matter of telling them what they need to do but of listening for the solutions to come out of their own mouth. Discern the solutions and restate them. This is called empathic listening. Empathic listening means that you must *really* listen. Do not furnish additional ideas or try to lead his thought process. Acknowledge what is being said and listen for additional details that will follow when the person feels that they are really being heard.

Discern what he is saying. Don't just listen to the words he says; read between the lines and interject encouragement where needed. A man takes awhile to open up, so when he does, put your own agenda aside and be attentive. What he says will reveal his concerns, his fears, and his ambitions. Ask a lot of questions. When was this interest birthed in him? Why is it important to him? What can you do to hold him accountable to achieving his dream?

Why did Jesus ask questions? Because ministry involves listening. You can't assist people until you locate them. Don't just be his audience; become his partner. Try to learn about what interests him so that you have comments to exchange on the subject. As he senses your genuine involvement in his dreams, he will share more and more with you. His heart will begin to trust you because he sees you as a help and not a hindrance.

How do you step from really hearing him to inspiring him to be all that he can be? The man's purpose or his dream is likely bigger than his present accomplishments. As he begins to share his heart with you, in addition to hearing him, you must express a belief in his ability to accomplish his vision. God calls those things that are not as if they were. Begin to talk about his life as if his dream were a certain destination. When doubt, fear, or discouragement arise, remind him that he has the strength to avoid petty distractions and to endure the potential obstacles. What we are talking about is support, encouragement, and adjustment. We are not talking about leading or pulling. The man must be able to feel his own victory. You must help him achieve his victory, not achieve his victory for him. Be the woman at his side, be his muse, be the impetus of his achievement. But never be his mentor.

Celebrating his vision will also help inspire him. Learning about and feeding him information concerning what he is working toward will feed his excitement. Think of ways to weave his dream into normal activities. Be cognizant of television programs, books, exhibits, magazines, and the like that elaborate on his interest. When purchasing birthday cards, gifts, and so on, keep the theme of his dreams in mind. All of these actions will endear you to a man because what is dear to him has become dear to you as well.

In encouraging a man to achieve his vision, help him determine small steps he can take to get started toward his dream. For example, help arrange his schedule to include research on this matter, or find or suggest books and sources of information that will equip him for reaching his goals. After he agrees that he should take certain steps toward his goal, gently hold him accountable. The reason so few dreams are fulfilled is because of the urgent versus the important equation. Be a big help by focusing him on the important issues in life that are not necessarily urgent. Help him keep first things first. Once he begins to act on his vision, celebrate every small victory. Be his greatest cheerleader. Urge him toward the finish line.

Next, appeal to all of his senses—sight, sound, smell, touch, and taste. Not only should a man like what he sees when he looks at you, he should also like what surrounds you. Are you able to make a house a home? Will you be able to create an oasis for him? Your present living situation should reflect your ability to do that. Don't wait until you have a husband to practice the fine art of homemaking. Your house should reflect a feminine touch that is appealing now. This does not require an outlandish budget, just attention to detail. Neatness and cleanliness can say much more than expensive furnishings and accessories. Creativity with what you have can go a long way. Your home says more about you than you can ever vocalize. Set the stage for love and hospitality. Make it a place where people look forward to coming. Let the atmosphere in your home exude peace and comfort, a wonderful getaway from the rest of the world. Make it a place that feels like home to him.

In your home let him always hear encouragement from you. Make your voice one that he wants to listen to free of attitude, free of the edge that sets a man on his guard. No man likes a woman who is constantly challenging, correcting, or confronting him. The Word of God talks about those who come bringing good news. It says that even their feet are considered lovely (see Isaiah 52:7, NASB). People love to hear them coming because they know they can expect to hear things that make them feel positive. Fill your home with music and your conversation with words that will be music to his ears.

Smell is a very subjective thing we mentioned briefly in our discussion about grooming. Remember that Esther had twelve months of baths and perfumes before meeting the king. The point is to exude sweetness from the inside out. Leave the fruit of the Spirit—all that good stuff we've referred to previously—wafting in the air as pleasant memories of you long after you've departed from his presence. Leave your sweetness on his mind.

There are ways to touch without getting physical. Touch him with your eyes, your demeanor, your softness. Your inner qualities should make him want to touch and embrace you, to take hold and contain all that you are. This is done in loving ways and by thoughtful actions. These "touches" move a man's heart and linger in his mind longer than a sexual encounter. You want him to think of you first as his most desired escape when he's had a hard day—simply because you touch him inwardly in a way that no one else can.

And finally taste. The world is not too far off when they voice the sentiment that the way to a man's heart is through his stomach, yet many women have forsaken the art of cooking and/or insisted on eating out. Think about it. Ask a man about his mother, and one of the first things he mentions is her cooking. He does so because this is a source of comfort to him. But being cooked for is also a sign to him of tremendous care.

There is something spiritual about cooking. It takes time to prepare a meal. It is not just an offering of food. It is a sacrifice, not just naturally, but spiritually as well. It is an offering of yourself. Of your love and care. It is an act of servanthood. We mentioned earlier that women are often found drawing water in Scripture. After the water would typically come the offering of a meal. A man must be ministered to from the inside out. A man responds to a woman who finds joy in serving him, not in the menial sense, but in willingness. Filling him inwardly moves his heart to serve her. It breaks down his defenses, makes him vulnerable to the one who is doing the serving and open to anything else that you might propose. Even God requested a burnt offering in times of old.

Many women cringe at the idea of serving because they feel they are no longer in control. But servers have more control because they are making an active choice to yield themselves for the good of others. Jesus served those he came to rescue and became Lord of all. Serving is the ultimate definition of love.

But let's discuss the issue of control in more detail. There is a thin line between serving, helping, or stabilizing someone versus controlling them. There is a difference between influence and control. There is a difference between a covering and a lid. A covering is meant to protect. A lid is meant to contain. It is not God's will that either of you should limit the other's potential. Instead, through your assistance and covering, potential should be released.

Don't *you* become controlling! There is no sorrier sight than seeing a broken emasculated man. He resents his woman but feels helpless to pull himself back into the driver's seat. She, on the other hand, resents the fact that he won't. Even though she is running everything, she really wants him to exert his manhood and rise to the occasion. She wants him to earn her respect. But men don't fight with women in this way. They abdicate their post instead.

If you want a man that you can respect, you must allow him to be a man. Though he should never control you, allow him to lead the relationship and feel that he is in charge. Women have become so independent that a man no longer feels needed. Since men are fixers, if they can't find anything to fix or anyone to help, they move on. As we mentioned before, a man has to see himself as part of the solution to your needs. He has to see you as an assignment in his life. If you rob him of that, he has nowhere to go. Part of getting a man to commit to you is feeding his need to be needed as well as desired. Be sensitive to moments when you can give up the reigns. Control the urge to say, "I can do it myself." It's wonderful to know that you can do it yourself. So do it yourself when he isn't around. When he is, let him handle it.

There is nothing helpless about letting a man handle something, but isn't it a good feeling when he does? Serve him and allow yourself to be served.

Things That Make You Go Hmmm...

* Do you recognize and understand the full scope of your power?

* Have you really listened to this man's heart?

* Do his vision and interests excite you?

* Do you have a desire to impress, help, or please him?

* Do you consider serving him beneath you? If so, why?

* Are you allowing him to be a man that you can respect?

Chapter Fourteen

Positioned to Receive

Rule #14: Close the Deal or the Door

When we talk about serving one's prospective mate, we need to revisit the concept of *balance*. It's important that you do not overcommit too early and become someone's wife functionally without being their wife in reality. Though we've given you several tips to his heart, you should never give him full servings of all that you can supply but merely appetizer portions. Give him only enough to whet his appetite for more. Keep it on the down low. In small and friendly ways, you can be that powerful force in his life at this stage of the relationship. You want him to come to the conclusion that, in order to have more of that good treatment on a regular basis, he is going to have to marry you. If you recall from the Rutgers University study asking why men won't commit, the second highest scoring answer was that men could enjoy the benefits of marriage without having to commit.

Christian women are famous for making a horrible mistake over and over again: They feel that God has spoken to them about a specific man. We *are not* saying that God will never speak to your heart about the man you are to marry, but we *are* saying that it is very dangerous for a woman to get hung up on a feeling. Especially if you see no concrete indication from the other person. What a person believes to be God's will for her, she will readily commit to. She makes it an issue of faith. When most women feel that they know God's will for their life, especially in this area, they commit to it ruthlessly and ignore any conflicting information—including wise counsel. Remember our second chapter? Guard yourself against creating false pictures of your future.

TWO-PARTY CONSENT

We want to help you guard against illusion. When you commit to a man based upon what you believe is a "word from the Lord," you will give him unqualified commitment and consider anything that speaks to the contrary as a test of your faith. You will hold on to this person even it they tell you to move on because you simply believe that they have not heard from God yet. A great tool is to remember that anytime God speaks concerning two people, he informs *both* parties involved. When God sent the angel to talk to Mary, the mother of Jesus, he also sent the angel to Joseph to tell him to marry Mary. Joseph heard and was obedient. If the man you are believing God for cannot hear from God to marry you, how will he hear from

God to lead you? Let's be realistic; it is very easy—too easy—to believe that God wants you to have something that you want anyway. You can avoid the disappointment that comes from trying to control in this unhealthy way by being honest with yourself and admitting strong attraction without spiritualizing it.

Here's another trap to avoid: Some women believe that, because the man they feel they are supposed to marry is not someone they would normally be attracted to, this is evidence of God's leading. We say no. This thought just speaks of a woman's wrong perception of God. The blessings of the Lord make rich and add no sorrow, meaning that a woman will desire and enjoy the things God brings into her life. As we mentioned previously, neither attraction nor lack of attraction is a basis for marriage.

THE RIGHT BALANCE

As the deal works toward closing, you must balance your service to the man in your life by holding him accountable for where the relationship is at a particular point and for where he sees it going. When you sense ambiguity from him, be honest with him and tell him where you are and that you think maybe you should pull back. Remember that people are very hesitant to give up options because loss of options is a loss. He needs to be conscious of the fact that keeping his options could cause him to lose you. These actions will require some risk on your part, of course, because he may take you up on your offer to pull back. At least you will know where you stand. You won't waste unnecessary months or even years giving to and serving a man in hopes that he will marry you, and you will surely avoid drawn-out disappointment and heartbreak.

In one case, a couple had been dating each other for a few years. They were close, loved each other, and had even become physically intimate (which you know by now we advise against prior to marriage), but he would not commit to her. Whenever she would bring up the subject of marriage, he would back-pedal and say he was not ready. In other words, he was ready to play house, but he was not ready to be a man. She was then persuaded to break up with him, and for a period of about year, he went crazy. He couldn't stand being without her. He called her, her friends, her relatives, his friends, and his relatives—driving everybody nuts—trying to get her back. When she finally allowed him back into her life, he promptly proposed. They are now happily married and doing just fine.

If all the circumstances we have described for a healthy bond are right, your relationship will move forward. But you don't want to end up in the situation we just described, so you need to ask him questions on a regular basis. You do this to locate where you are with him. You don't do this as an effort to put pressure on him or to change him. You simply ask questions, not overstating your case, to figure out where you stand. You need to know so that you can determine your next move. Here are some suggestions: "Where are we? How do you feel about us? Where do you feel we are headed? What kind of timetable do you see for us?"

Be sure you don't ask these questions on a second date, or you might not get dessert, and you definitely won't get a third date. These questions are for a relationship that has evolved from friendship and grown considerably. Also, he will probably find your questions more palatable when you've first allowed some quality interaction to take place. If he is showing a physical interest in you, then it is a good time to ask these questions. We do not recommend asking them before, because you might be setting him up with a convenient way to back-peddle and say, "But we're just friends!" If, however, he is behaving as though he is your boyfriend, you should be able to ask. If you are both getting intimate in conversation or otherwise, if the relationship is monopolizing a lot of your time, if he is expecting exclusivity from you, then it's time to pull up and ask questions that keep him accountable for his actions.

Again, balance is the key. If you don't get the answer you're looking for, he needs to know that he can lose you. Let him know how long you will wait for him and how long you won't. Some men need deadlines. No man should be able to receive all the benefits of being married without the cost of commitment. A man may be in love with you, enjoy your presence, and still grapple with his fear of commitment. Make him fear something more—losing you.

Tell him honestly, "I'm really attracted to you. I find myself even falling in love with you, but since you have no vision for us, I am uncomfortable with my feelings for you. I am sensing a need for us to spend less time together or maybe stop seeing each other altogether. Perhaps we need to go our separate ways until you are at a different point in your life. Or maybe I need to allow you to find the person you can commit to. At this stage of my life, it is important to me that I find someone willing to commit to me. Continuing as we are prevents both of us from doing that."

The thought of not having you available to him as he has grown used to will be painful to him and will force him to rethink the answers he gave you. If you are all the things to him we have been talking about, he is not readily going to give you up. But if it turns out that he is prepared to give you up, then either you don't mean as much to him as you thought you did, or he is really not prepared to be married. In any case, the sooner you move on the better for you. Face the pain, and walk through it. Do not allow a man to put you on indefinite hold. Do not allow a man to hang around in your life, week after week, month after month, year after year, without stating where the relationship is going. If he says, "We are just friends," you must take what he says at face value and believe him.

The challenge for you is that there is a thin line between holding him accountable and pressuring him to marrying you. Don't pressure him. Allow the relationship to evolve naturally at a pace that works for him—but not at the sacrifice of your own comfort level. Don't allow yourself to commit your heart to him if he has not asked you to.

THE GAME OF LOVE

Colossians 3:15 says to "let the peace of Christ rule in your hearts." Another translation of this verse urges you to allow peace to be the referee or umpire in your heart. This makes sense if you have ever been to a baseball game. The player hits the ball and takes off running. The fielder catches the ball and throws it to first base. The runner and ball get there at the same time. The fans who are rooting for the runner insist that he was safe. Those rooting for the defensive team insist that he was out. Both believe what they saw.

The point is, what you *want* has a lot to do with what you *see*. If you want this person to be right for you, you tend to only see things that confirm your feelings. But if you allow peace to be the umpire, your heart will be able to rest in the fact that at the right time the right man will declare his love and commitment for you. That peace will enable you to see things as they really are and make the right call on your relationship.

When the runner and the ball have arrived at the base at the same time, no matter what the fans believe they saw, the umpire gives a signal for either safe or out. If you do not have peace about the person you are thinking about marrying, you need to declare them out. Unrest is the Holy Spirit trying to tell you that your heart is not safe with this person. You should not marry him in this case, even if he appears to be perfect for you. He is possibly the right person, but perhaps it is the wrong time. The bottom line: If you do not have peace, then something is wrong. You must wait!

Once again, this brings us back to the concept of being whole. You will know the peace of God about marriage if you have peace in general. If peace isn't a regular aspect of your life, will you know when it leaves? When the right person enters your life, your peace will remain. When the wrong person enters, your peace will leave.

Guard against mistaking passion for peace. Exercising patience and keeping your boundaries intact will give you a peace. Patience, the weapon that forces deception to reveal itself, will help you. Something may look right but be wrong. Or a person may have deficiencies but actually be the man of your future. Keep in mind that you are working out a balance between your head and your heart. You might have peace about someone whose circumstances are not ideal at the moment because they may be great in the future. Give him time and see what happens. Make sure that your head and your heart are in agreement. And make sure that he has asked for a commitment from you before you commit to him.

Last but not least, a crucial factor you must be aware of and know how to respond to is called Clanging Gate Syndrome. The man might pull back for a moment when faced with the enormity of what a commitment to you really means. Or he might do something absolutely ridiculous to anger you and put distance between the two of you. Do not go off, throw a tantrum, or confront him. Quietly retreat and, in so doing, let him know that this sort of behavior is neither something you will tolerate nor respond to. When he is serious, he can let you know. In the meantime, life goes on.

If you do not pursue him and simply carry on with your life, he will be back. We repeat, *he will be back*. When he returns, do not allow him to resume his normal routine in your life. If he is in the habit of calling at a certain time, do not always be available. Do not let him monopolize you again. Be happy to see him, fit him into your schedule, but do not allow him to fill it. You must not let him return to his comfort zone with you. He must come to the conclusion that if he wants you back on his schedule, he has to marry you.

Now! You are a whole person. You've had your attractions adjusted. You've been honest with yourself about the man in your life and his intentions toward you. You've protected your heart, maintained your value, and cultivated all of your feminine gifts. You've collected all the data you need on this man, and he has passed all the tests. Now is not the time to relax or try to push the issue over the edge. Use your head, stay cool, let peace reign. Maintain your mystery. Leave just enough room for him to have to reach. Distract him from all of his other options by not being overly available. Keep him slightly off balance by not allowing him to establish a routine with you. Set the bar for his leap of faith into the world of commitment. Sit back as he lands at your feet. Then smile your most brilliant smile and say, "Yes."

Reading List

Stephen Arterburn and Dr. Meg J. Rinck, *Avoiding Mr. Wrong (and What to Do if You Didn't)* and *Finding Mr. Right (and How to Know When You Have)*

Edwin Louis Cole, *Maximized Manhood: A Guide to Family Survival*

Barbara De Angelis, Ph.D., *Are You the One for Me? Knowing Who's Right and Avoiding Who's Wrong*

Laurie Beth Jones, *The Path: Creating Your Mission Statement for Work and for Life*

E. W. Kenyon, *The Hidden Man: An Unveiling of the Subconscious Mind*

Michelle McKinney Hammond, *If Men are Like Buses, Then How Do I Catch One?*; *Secrets of an Irresistible Woman*; and *What To Do Until Love Finds You*

Susan Page, *If I'm So Wonderful, Why Am I Still Single? Ten Strategies That Will Change Your Love Life Forever*

Neil Clark Warren, Ph.D., *Date...or Soul Mate? How to Know if Someone Is Worth Pursuing in Two Dates or Less* and *Finding the Love of Your Life: Ten Principles for Choosing the Right Marriage Partner*

P. B. Wilson, *Knight in Shining Armor: Discovering Your Lifelong Love*

Acknowledgments

I would like to thank my family for bearing with me during the writing of this book. Joel, Victoria, and Veronica, you are my heart.

I would also like to thank my staff, especially Alva, Donna, Erika, Steve, Brian, and Claudia for assisting me when I was under the gun; also Ervin and Carl for keeping the church on course as I stretched out to work on other projects.

To my mentor, the late Dr. Edwin Louis Cole, who poured into my life and taught me what being a man was all about. Your legacy is the army of men whose lives you have affected so deeply. I am proud to be one of them, and I miss you very much.

To my pastor, Joseph Garlington Sr., thank you for inviting me into your home to jump-start this project. That day with you got me over the hump. Your impact in my life is immeasurable, and I believe our best days are still ahead of us.

These two men have had such an impact on my life that if you know them you will hear them throughout this book.

I would also like to thank another single male comrade, Mike Murdock. Mike, your wisdom continues to inspire me. I consider you a friend and a mentor.

Most of all, I would like to thank Michelle McKinney Hammond for proposing this project, then prodding and coaxing me into finishing it. You are a blessing to so many people and a significant blessing to me. I am very honored to have you as a friend. I cannot thank you enough.

Finally, a special thank you to my parents for having me and for raising me.

God bless you all.

—*Joel A. Brooks Jr.*

I must thank WaterBrook Press for having the passion to reach out to women of color. I am so pleased and blessed to be a part of your family. Don, Laura, John, Kirsten, and all who make it happen, you are amazing, and I love you dearly.

Joel Brooks, you are an amazing man and wonderful friend. I've learned so much from you. You are a gift in my life, and I feel privileged to be your partner in this very special offering.

Adrian Ingram, thank you for your hard work and encouragement. Laura Wright, thank you for always focusing me. You are a gem.

To all the men that have shared their heart with me over the years and given me insight into the male psyche (you know who you are). My dear "brothers," Daryll Merchant, Jeff Morrow, and Dwayne Bryant, your friendship has been priceless.

—*Michelle McKinney Hammond*

About the Authors

Joel A. Brooks Jr. is a nationally known speaker and senior pastor of Christian Life Center, a dynamic 1,600-member multicultural church located in Kalamazoo, Michigan, with regularly televised services throughout Western Michigan.

In a segregating nation, Pastor Brooks has made a strong stand for racial reconciliation and unity. He places an emphasis on men taking the leadership role for which God created them. He also targets young adults, challenging them to mature and to accept responsibility.

Pastor Brooks serves on many local and national boards, including Reconciliation Ministries and the Christian Men's Network. He is also the president and founder of Romantic Warrior Ministries.

He is a featured author of a chapter in Dr. Edwin Louis Cole's book *Man Power*. Walking in the company of such men as Ed Cole, Joseph Garlington, and Mike Murdock has given him a rich overflow of wisdom to serve to others in the area of relationships, as well as a sound perspective on godly womanhood and manhood. He brings his teachings for this book from a series taught at his church as well as from singles seminars throughout the country.

Michelle McKinney Hammond, founder of HeartWing Ministries, is a vibrant author and speaker. She has been a keynote speaker at the Women of Virtue conferences and Focus on the Family events. She also speaks regularly at women's retreats, universities, and church services.

Michelle is cohost of *Aspiring Women,* the Chicago-based, syndicated, Emmy-nominated television talk show. She has been featured on the cover of several women's magazines in the past two years, including *Today's Christian Woman, Excellence,* and *Plain Truth,* and has been a guest on *Politically Incorrect,* BET's *Oh Drama,* NBC's *The Other Half, The James Robison Show,* TBN, *The 700 Club, 100 Huntley Street, It's a New Day, Herman and Sharon,* and several others. Michelle is also a nationally recognized voiceover talent for radio and television commercials.

Michelle is also the author of more than fifteen books including:

What to Do Until Love Finds You
Secrets of an Irresistible Woman
If Men Are Like Buses, Then How Do I Catch One?
The Power of Femininity
Sassy, Single, and Satisfied
Get Over It and On With It
How to Be Blessed and Highly Favored
Why Do I Say Yes When I Need to Say No?
What Becomes of the Brokenhearted?
Prayer Guide for the Brokenhearted